The Distance Learner's Guide

Western Cooperative for Educational Telecommunications

George P. Connick
Editor

Prentice Hall
Upper Saddle River, New Jersey 07458

Library of Congress Cataloging-in-Publication Data

The distance learner's guide / Western Cooperative for Educational
   Telecommunications : George P. Connick, editor.
        p.   cm.
     Includes index.
     ISBN 0-13-939513-X
     1. Distance education.   2. Distance education—Computer-assisted
   instruction.   I. Connick, George P.   II. Western Cooperative for
   Educational Telecommunications.
   LC5800.D578   1999
   371.3'5—dc21   98-27155
                                                                       CIP

Publisher: *Carol Carter*
Acquisitions Editor: *Sue Bierman*
Managing Editor: *Mary Carnis*
Production Management/Interior Design: *Holcomb Hathaway, Inc.*
Production Liaison: *Adele M. Kupchik*
Director of Manufacturing and Production: *Bruce Johnson*
Manufacturing Buyer: *Marc Bove*
Creative Director: *Marianne Frasco*
Cartoon Illustrations: *Mark Ammerman, North Market Street Graphics*
Cover Design: *Bruce Kenselaar*
Typesetting: *Aerocraft Charter Art Service*
Editorial Assistant: *Amy Diehl*
Marketing Manager: *Jeff McIlroy*
Marketing Assistant: *Barbara Rosenberg*
Printer/Binder: *R. R. Donnelley & Sons, Harrisonburg, VA*
Cover Illustration: *Coco Masuda*
WebMaster: *Patrick Walsh*
Web Site Design: *Steve Hartner, Martha Bray*

Printed in the United States of America

10 9 8 7 6 5 4 3 2 1

ISBN 0-13-939513-X

Prentice-Hall International (UK) Limited, *London*
Prentice-Hall of Australia Pty. Limited, *Sydney*
Prentice-Hall Canada Inc., *Toronto*
Prentice-Hall Hispanoamericana, S.A., *Mexico*
Prentice-Hall of India Private Limited, *New Delhi*
Prentice-Hall of Japan, Inc., *Tokyo*
Simon & Schuster Asia Pte. Ltd., *Singapore*
Editora Prentice-Hall do Brasil, Ltda., *Rio de Janeiro*

Tips for Using This Guide and the Companion Web Site

How to Use the Guide

If you are a **first-time college student,** you should read the entire Guide, beginning with Chapter 1. Each chapter of the Guide will add to your knowledge and understanding of both higher education and distance learning.

If you are a **returning college student** who has taken courses on a campus, you should concentrate on Chapters 1 through 4. You will find that the policies and procedures of distance learning are substantially different than those on a campus. You will also find the chapters on student services and career planning (Chapters 5–7) of assistance, but they can be deferred until you have specific questions that need to be answered.

And, finally, if you are a **former distance learning student,** you should focus on Chapters 2 through 4, which will assist you in making good choices about future distance learning opportunities and the academic support you will need.

How to Use the Companion Web Site

This Guide is supported by a wealth of material on a companion Web site that may be found at:

http://www.prenhall.com/dlguide

Organized the same as the Guide, the Web site offers material that expands and amplifies what has been covered in each chapter. You will find a list of more than 900 providers of distance education, a variety of helpful forms, suggestions for additional reading, and much more. Whenever you see this symbol in the book, check the companion Web site for additional information on the topic being discussed.

Brief Contents

Contents

DISTANCE LEARNING

THE DISTANCE LEARNER'S LIBRARY

The Indispensable Guide to Finding the Material   69

UNDERSTANDING YOUR NEEDS

Overcoming the Personal Barriers to Success in Distance Learning   89

IMPROVING DISTANCE LEARNING PERFORMANCE

6

Steps to Success   111

CAREER PLANNING

Building a Personal Life Plan 145

Foreword

In the past three years the number of college courses offered to students on the Internet and World Wide Web has increased exponentially. This has contributed to the overall growth of distance learning in all forms. The Western Cooperative for Educational Telecommunications (WCET) works to encourage these types of opportunities for students. It also works with colleges and universities to ensure that the students who choose to study electronically receive not only high-quality instruction but also good support services. As part of that effort, we encourage colleges and universities to think about students as consumers and give them the level of service that consumers of education should expect.

As colleges and universities begin to treat students as consumers, it is critical that the students understand how to be "informed" consumers. That is what this book is all about. Through many years of research and interviews with students and their instructors, we know that students studying in an electronic environment must take more control over their learning than might be the case for students in a face-to-face class situation.

This book is designed to empower students and to help them understand how to be informed consumers of electronically mediated learning and, consequently, more successful in this new environment.

Sally M. Johnstone, Director
Western Cooperative for Educational Telecommunications

Preface

The drawing on the opposite page is a wonderful modern illustration of Aesop's 2500-year-old fable about the tortoise and the hare. As you will recall, the tortoise and the hare argued about who could run faster, and the hare challenged the tortoise to a race. At the beginning of the race, the hare was quickly ahead and became bored. He stopped to rest and soon fell asleep. The tortoise plodded along without stopping, focused on her goal. Just as the hare awoke, the tortoise crossed the finish line. The moral of this fable is that "slow and steady wins the race."

This lesson applies to education as well as racing. There are no shortcuts and no instant returns on your educational investment.

This Guide is designed to help you reach your educational goals. It is about a world of higher education that is new, expanding rapidly, and accessible from home, work, or other locations distant from a campus. In other words, it is about what is termed *distance learning*.

Where the traditional college experience takes place on a campus at a specific time each week, you, as a distance learner, will access your courses in a "virtual educational world" at times and places convenient to you.

Distance learning has expanded dramatically as a result of amazing developments in computers, telecommunications, the Internet, and the World Wide Web. The merging of these technologies has resulted in an "information technology revolution" and has made possible the rapid expansion of distance learning options. Today, distance learning is a new educational culture with its own distinct characteristics.

As you search for distance learning opportunities, you will find this Guide valuable in several important ways.

First, it is designed to help you understand and successfully navigate every avenue of this new "virtual culture" in higher education. Written by experts in distance learning, each chapter is full of detailed information about degree programs and services available at a distance.

Secondly, it is the first book that provides comprehensive guidance in the areas essential for success in distance learning. It will help you find the distance education provider that offers the degree

program that you need, use a computer for distance learning, access library resources from a distance, and secure a wide range of student services without traveling to a campus.

Finally, it is much more than a book. It is a dynamic learning tool, combining the written word with the interactive capabilities of the Internet and the World Wide Web. The Guide directs you to locations on the Web where there are vast quantities of supplementary material for each chapter. Wherever you see this Web symbol, it indicates that there is additional information on the companion Web site at

http://www.prenhall.com/dlguide

related to the topic being discussed. Because the Web site is routinely updated, the Guide remains current.

New distance learning opportunities appear daily. This Guide, with its companion Web site, will help you locate the classes or degree program that is best and most convenient for you.

CHAPTER 1

DISTANCE LEARNING

The Instructional Strategy of the Decade

In this chapter you will

- ◆ learn how to use this Guide
- ◆ learn about the concept of distance learning
- ◆ become familiar with some terms used to discuss distance learning
- ◆ discover some reasons why people are taking advantage of distance learning to meet their goals
- ◆ learn what it might be like to experience a distance learning course
- ◆ find out more about how the quality of distance learning is likely to compare to that of a traditional learning experience
- ◆ be given some tools to help you evaluate whether distance learning is for you

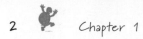

THE PURPOSE OF THE GUIDE

This book is a comprehensive guide to the complex world of distance learning. It is designed to provide you with a broad understanding of this emerging field of distance learning and also to advise you on the issues that are key to your success as a distance learner. Unlike a novel, it is not designed to be read from cover to cover in one sitting. However, we believe that you will find it compelling reading as you explore the issues essential to your future success as a distance learner.

ORGANIZATION OF THE GUIDE

The Guide is organized into four sections. These sections represent the stages that students pass through as they access distance learning opportunities.

1. Chapter 1 introduces you to distance learning. It discusses new terms and concepts that are at the core of the distance learning experience.

2. Chapters 2 through 4 focus on the academic issues that are essential to your success as a distance learner—how to choose the institution that best fits your personal needs, how to ensure that you have the appropriate computer support, and how to access library and other learning resources.

3. Chapters 5 and 6 cover student support issues that are extremely important to the success of every distance learner. We often underestimate the importance of personal issues in our ultimate success as learners. If our personal lives are not in order, it is much more difficult to succeed in the highly structured world of education.

4. Chapter 7 moves you from the academic world to the world of work by helping you plan the transition from college to career. It is included in this Guide to encourage you to think routinely about the ways in which your educational experiences prepare you for your career choice and how you organize your resources to secure the job you want.

WHAT IS DISTANCE LEARNING?

A reasonable first question. The term *distance learning* is heard everywhere, but it's hard to know exactly what it is because it is defined in different ways. Perhaps the simplest definition is that distance learning takes place when the instructor and student are not in the same room but instead are separated by physical distance.

But the "distance" in the term doesn't imply any particular degree of separation. You can be a distant learner located only a short hop across campus from the instructor, or you can be thousands of miles away—across the continent or in another country. Whatever the physical space between the student and teacher, they are connected to each other by video, voice, or computer technologies.

Distance learning is a flexible form of education because it creates options in terms of where and when you can learn. As a distant learner, you may learn with others in a group gathered in a classroom at an off-campus site, or you may learn on your own from your computer at home, communicating with other students and your instructor only in a "virtual" space.

Other Terms for Distance Learning

- *Distance education* is a term that is often used interchangeably with distance learning. When you think about it, though, distance learning might best be seen as what takes place *as a result of* distance education.

- *Distributed education* is a term that has recently become prominent. It is often used to describe programs where courses are taught online and collaboration and "virtual interaction" among students in the same course are encouraged.

WHO OFFERS DISTANCE LEARNING PROGRAMS?

Many kinds of providers are offering distance learning programs. In addition to traditional colleges and universities, providers include small and large businesses, government agencies, nonprofit organizations, and for-profit entities formed specifically to offer distance learning opportunities.

This handbook is designed especially for students interested in distance learning opportunities that are made available through **traditional higher education institutions,** both public and private:

- community colleges
- four-year colleges
- universities that award four-year and graduate and professional degrees

- consortia comprised of groups of higher education institutions

ONLINE AND VIRTUAL UNIVERSITIES

The terms *virtual university* and *online university* turn up when distance learning is discussed. What are these institutions? Are they real places?

- An online university is likely to be an offshoot of a traditional institution. Remember, however, that it takes more than a home page on the Web to make an online university. An online university offers all its courses and programs via the Internet or World Wide Web. Examples are the New School for Social Research's distance learning program and the Online Campus of the University of Phoenix.
- A virtual university has no campus and no faculty of its own. Instead, a virtual university makes available programs and courses offered by other colleges and universities using technology. The Western Governors University and the California Virtual University are two examples of virtual universities.

WHY STUDY AT A DISTANCE?

Students enroll in distance learning programs for a variety of reasons. Usually they are interested in the convenience such programs offer—the possibility of earning college credits at a local community site, at home, or at work and the flexibility built into most programs. The greatest appeal of distance learning is that you can study without having to leave home or a job to go to campus. Perhaps you live in a rural area or are caring for young children. Or you have a full-time job but need to get an advanced degree. Or you need education to enter a new career field. Or you want to get a two-year degree now and may transfer to a four-year program later. Maybe you are physically disabled and would find it hard to get to a campus.

Distance learning is not for everyone. But some people find distance learning the perfect way to fit an educational pursuit into their busy lives. Once you understand all your options, you can decide if distance learning is for you.

DISTANCE LEARNING: HOW QUICKLY IT CHANGES

Distance learning is not a new concept. Today's distance learning programs are descendants of the correspondence courses that were first offered early in the 20th century and are still available today. Correspondence courses rely on written course materials sent through the mail, while most distance education courses now use technology to deliver some or all of the course materials and to convey instruction.

The technologies used in distance learning have evolved rapidly. Radio was used to deliver education at a distance in the first half of the 20th century, and in the 1950s, local educational television stations developed. The Public Broadcasting Service's telecourses were seen everywhere from the 1960s to the 1980s. At that point, interactive video technologies began to gain popularity. Telecourses and video are still widely used, but in the 1990s, computer and multimedia technologies have become the latest telecommunications media used in distance learning.

Distance learning has seen enormous growth since the mid-1990s. A recent U. S. Department of Education study based on data from 1994–95 reported that three-quarters of large higher education institutions and two-thirds of medium-size institutions were then offering courses or programs at a distance; these proportions have grown steadily since then. Today, about 75 percent of colleges and universities are offering distance learning courses or programs, and another 10 percent of both large and medium-size institutions plan to do so in the future.

TECHNOLOGY-SUPPORTED LEARNING

The opportunities made available by new technologies are changing not only distance learning but learning on campus as well. In fact,

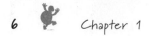

technology-supported learning is blurring the distinction between distance learning and any learning that relies exclusively on technological media. Technology is allowing students—both on and off campus—to take more responsibility for their learning.

In today's technology-based environment, you may find that education is becoming more learner-centered than teacher-centered. This learner-centered approach focuses on creating an environment in which you, as learner, can be actively involved in your learning instead of passively absorbing information conveyed by the instructor.

TECHNOLOGIES USED IN DISTANCE EDUCATION

To become a distance learner, you don't need to be an expert in the varieties of instructional technology being used today. In fact, almost all distance learning technologies are based on one or a combination of just three media: telephone, video, and computer.

Telephone

- **Audioconferencing** enables participants at multiple sites to use telephones to communicate with each other.
- **Audiographics** uses a combination of voice and data communications. Students can speak with the instructor and students at other sites and, via computer, can view graphics and pictures developed by the instructor. In addition, students may also be able to use an electronic pen and tablet to mark on the visuals, as on a board in a regular classroom.
- **Fax** allows students and faculty to send materials electronically or on paper over phone lines.
- **Voice mail** gives students a way to reach faculty and other students by leaving phone messages.

Video

- **Telecourses** are taped or live television programs carried by broadcast or cable television stations. A study guide for each course provides directions and assignments to students.
- **Videotapes** are videos recorded during a class period or tapes reproduced especially for a distance learning class. They can be

viewed later by a student via his TV and videocassette recorder (VCR) at home.

- **One-way video** transmits live video signals in one direction: from the instructor to learners. (The basic technology can be Instructional Fixed Television Service (IFTS),—cable or satellite.) Students can receive the video transmission in a classroom or through a desktop videoconferencing unit. During the class period, off-site students can communicate with the instructor over the phone or through a return key.

- **Interactive video** systems equip two or more locations with cameras, monitors, and microphones, enabling those at the origin site and those in off-site classrooms to see and hear each other.

Computer

- Stand-alone computer-based programs deliver self-paced instruction via CD-ROM, diskette, or connection to a local area or wide area network.

- Internet-based education requires a student to have a computer connected to the Internet, which links computers all over the world. A variety of tools are then available.

  - The World Wide Web is like having the largest library and entertainment center in the world at your fingertips.

  - Electronic mail (email) enables instructors and students to communicate quickly across time and distance by typing messages to each other.

- Some recent applications have increased the interactivity of the Web and created collaborative virtual work spaces for student–student and student–instructor interactivity. These applications make it possible for you to work cooperatively on projects with other students, no matter how far apart geographically you are.

  - Java (an animation program, not coffee) can make Web pages come alive with animation features similar to that usually found on CD-ROMs.

  - Streaming audio lets Web users hear a sound file while they view a picture of the person speaking when the file was made.

  - Computer conferencing can be set up either as real-time "chat" spaces so that participants can interact at the same time or as

systems that do not require participants to be present at the same time.

- GroupWare packages create an "electronic work space" for collaborative efforts and group processes.

Always, just over the horizon, is a new technology or software package with the potential to change the face of distance learning in yet another way—and probably to enhance learning as well.

WHICH TECHNOLOGY IS BEST?

The technologies used in distance learning are enablers. They are only tools, not the real point of distance learning. What really matters is how engaged you are in your learning experiences. The more involved and active you are, the more you will learn.

No single technology is best for distance learning. The technology that is most appropriate for one course or one student may be totally unsuitable for another. The best distance learning experiences, in fact, may be those that combine a variety of technologies for different purposes. For example, you may find that a course offered via two-way (interactive) video also includes an email component to encourage students' interaction outside class with each other and the instructor.

Your own situation gives you some clues about what technological media (and therefore what specific courses) are available to you. If a course is offered via videotape, for example, and you don't have access to a VCR, the course won't do you much good. If you don't have access to a computer, you can't enroll in an online course.

SYNCHRONOUS VERSUS ASYNCHRONOUS COMMUNICATION: A CRUCIAL DIFFERENCE

There are two basic ways of thinking about distance learning. The terms *synchronous communication* and *asynchronous communication* explain the essential differences by defining the extent to which a course is bounded by place and/or time.

Synchronous communication is communication in which all parties participate at the same time. Synchronous communication in distance learning emphasizes a simultaneous group learning experience. Teachers and students communicate in "real time," usually via interactive audio- or videoconferencing from a classroom to one or more remote classrooms. If you take a course that uses synchronous conferencing communication, you must attend at a specified time and in a specified place.

Synchronous communication may also be thought of as an extended classroom—even if the "classroom" is your bedroom at your computer workstation. Media used for synchronous delivery include interactive audio and video, audiographics, and some GroupWare applications, such as online "chat rooms" in which students communicate via the computer at the same time but from different places.

Asynchronous communication is communication in which parties participate at different times. Asynchronous communication offers a choice of where and, above all, *when* you will access learning. In a class using asynchronous communication, you can learn any time and any place you choose. Web-based courses belong to this category, as do videotapes, email, Listservs, and correspondence courses. In an asynchronous course, the instructor usually posts on the Internet the lesson materials and assignments for the course. You may read or view these materials at your own convenience. After you have completed the assigned activities, you send (via computer, fax, or regular mail) your completed work to the instructor for evaluation.

Since you study and do the course work on your own time, wherever it is convenient, asynchronous classes might seem to emphasize only individual learning. However, asynchronous learning can also be a group experience. In this type of learning, the interactions with your instructor and fellow students don't take place in "real time," that is, simultaneously. Instead, each of you works at your own pace, contributing to a group discussion by posting comments on the computer or even by leaving each other voice mail messages.

You'll find as many variations among distance learning classes as you've no doubt experienced among regular classrooms. This makes distance learning hard to generalize. The two examples presented next offer at least a general idea of what it might be like for you to take part in two common versions of distance learning classes.

Synchronous Communication: An Extended Classroom

Where and When. You attend class sessions at a specific time and place—often three times a week, but at least once a week. The instructor is located—along with the "on-site students"—in a classroom on campus. You are likely to be in one of several groups gathered at various off-campus sites—at places such as public libraries, community colleges, cooperative extension offices, or regional learning centers near where you live or work. Often, videotapes of televised classes are available for student use and review later.

The Experience. The "feel of the class" depends partly on the technology used. There's an obvious difference, of course, between the experience of a class delivered via audioconference (where you can only hear each other) and one that uses two-way video (where you can also see each other). But in all cases, you and the other off-site students will be able to participate in the class as it is taking place—in real time.

In a class using two-way video, the sound and picture on the video screen may or may not—again, depending on the exact technology used—be as smoothly coordinated as in a regular broadcast television show. Everyone's movements may look a bit jerky, and there might be a brief delay between the sound of a speaker's voice and the picture of the person speaking. However, you'll be able to see and hear the on-site students and the teacher and they can see and hear you. If a technical problem crops up during the class, there usually will be a local technician there to fix it.

Tests. Classes taught via distance learning technologies face a special problem when it comes to exam time. To be fair to all students in the course, your instructor must make sure that the person taking the test is actually the one enrolled. One way to handle this is to require everyone to come to campus for exams. This may be unfair, or impractical, especially if the students in the course are widely dispersed. Colleges often appoint off-site proctors to check the identity of students. In two-way video classes, the instructor can see students in the remote classroom whenever the camera pans the room. Some faculty rely on this method of ensuring exam integrity, while others feel more comfortable having exam proctors at each off-site location.

Faculty–Student Interaction Outside Class. As a distance learner, you may not be able to talk to your instructor in person during her office hours. This does not mean you are cut off from contact between class periods. Your instructor will make clear on the course syllabus some specific times and ways for you to ask questions and contact her outside of class. If you have access to email, you may be able to contact your instructor easily through that means. If you don't have email, your instructor may give you a phone number (sometimes toll-free) or a fax number. So even from a distance, you should be able to get the help you need.

Student Interaction Outside Class. Students who take a class together in a local community often form close learning groups. You might meet with a group for coffee to study together or you may exchange phone numbers; therefore, if you miss a class session, you'll be able to contact someone to catch up with assignments. The instructor may, in addition, set up optional computer-based mailing lists ("Listservs") or chat groups to enable you and the students from other sites to communicate with each other.

Asynchronous Communication: As It Suits You

The most important feature of an asynchronous course is that you can take it wherever and whenever it suits you. Although the following description is of an online Web-based course, remember that asynchronous courses may be offered on videotape, audiotape, or even through correspondence.

Where and When. Anywhere, any time. The instructor puts learning materials on the Internet, and you and other students may access these materials at any time before the assignment is due. You can study at home, in your workplace, a hotel room while you're traveling on business—wherever it's convenient.

You may be able to use your computer to register online for a course or program, order books, or complete applications for financial aid. Some online courses may offer scheduled synchronous possibilities, such as chat rooms, where a teacher and students arrange to be online at the same time.

The Experience. The materials for the class probably will be organized in electronic folders according to date; they can be designed for everyone in the class or personalized for individual students. Information can be linked to additional resources on the Web. Most online courses emphasize collaboration and communication, often using Web-based message systems to connect students with each other and the instructor.

It might seem that studying online would make you feel isolated from the rest of the class and the instructor. However, students report that they feel *more* connected to the class than they did in a traditional classroom. People often find that they are drawn into the subject matter of a class because of the online discussions they participate in with their peers and instructor.

Tests.   Many online courses are designed so that there are no conventional "tests." Instead, instructors rely on a series of writing assignments, open-book exams, and/or problem-solving assignments to gauge a student's progress through a course. The issue of exam integrity is a difficult one when everyone is working on a computer at home. There is no real way to guarantee that the work submitted online is really the work of the enrolled student. A number of online security systems have been developed, which require every user to log on with a user name and a password. However, even these systems cannot ensure that the only person in the room is the enrolled student. Therefore, many online courses are run on the honor system, and others actually encourage collaborative work among groups of students, who are then evaluated together.

Faculty–Student Interaction Outside the Course.   Online classes offer many ways for students and instructors to communicate. Since every student in the class obviously has access to a computer and the Internet, instructors can set up a variety of computer-based methods for communication. In addition to regular email, these might include online discussions or interactions.

Student Interaction Outside the Course.   In many online classes, the instructor encourages students to work together on projects even though they live far apart from each other and have different schedules. Packages of learning materials make this kind of collaborative effort possible, and online chat rooms facilitate discussions among class members. In other classes, students may work more independently, relying on email to communicate with each other.

WHO ARE DISTANCE LEARNERS?

Most distance learners are over 25 years old, have a job, and have previously completed some education beyond high school. About 60 percent are women. Distance learners are people who—because of time, place, or other constraints—choose not to pursue their educational goals in a traditional on-campus setting.

Distance learners have many different backgrounds and educational goals. They include adults returning to college, first-time students, mid-career professionals seeking continuing education, workers obtaining a credential to make a job change possible, students with physical and learning disabilities, and geographically isolated students. Here are a few examples:

Sarah L. lives in Chicago where she works full-time as a teller at a large bank downtown. For the last three years, she has been taking classes to complete her bachelor's degree in accounting, so she can move into the accounting department in the bank. Until she began taking videotaped courses, her progress to complete her degree had been slow. She is a divorced mother with two children—ages three and six—and balancing work, child care, and school made it difficult to attend even a single course each semester at any of the many colleges in Chicago. The flexibility of videotaped courses has made it possible for Sarah to finish 12 credit hours in the last year. Sarah watches the preproduced video lectures and does her assignments at home in the evening after her children are in bed and on alternate weekends when they are visiting their father. She interacts with her professor and other students using a sophisticated voice mail system.

Lauren and Robert F. are orthopedic surgeons at a large hospital in Rhode Island. They have worked together at the same hospital for the last 16 years. For most of that time, they have struggled to fit required continuing education courses into their demanding schedules, alternating evenings with the children and nights on call to drive to seminars and classes. Last year, Lauren attended a lecture about the benefits of online learning and tried her first course, which was offered by a top medical school. "In a profession where an average of 20 continuing education credits are required every two years, online learning really makes sense," Lauren says. Robert agrees: "The Web is the perfect medium for the dynamic field of medicine."

Michael J. needs a bachelor's degree to advance profession-ally, but he lives in a small town in eastern Oregon, quite distant from the nearest higher education institution offering four-year degrees. After a bit of investigating, he found that Eastern Oregon University offers an External Degree in Liberal Studies at regional centers throughout the eastern portion of the state. Michael has enrolled in the program, which uses a satellite-based video net-work to deliver courses at a center near his home. He has been pleased with the quality of the courses he has taken and also with the one-to-one help he has received from the regional center's coordinator, who has helped him plan his program, semester by semester, to com-pletion. Michael now has only three more courses to finish before receiving his degree.

Paul R. is living in Milan, Italy, where his wife Emma is complet-ing her active duty in the military. Paul is a freelance photographer and is used to traveling. He took his first online course when they lived in Frankfurt, Germany, a few years ago and has continued to take a course each semester. He has always liked learn-ing, but Emma's career has made it difficult for him to enroll in traditional university courses. In the past two years, she has been assigned to new posts three times. Most of the time the nearest univer-sity hasn't offered the courses he wants to take in English. Initially, Paul was worried because he didn't know a lot about computers, but he found the courses had been designed for new users. For Paul online courses are fun. In addition, he has found that online courses give him a link to the United States and provide him with a real, if virtual, com-munity, which isn't always easy to find abroad.

Characteristics of Successful Distance Learners

Those who succeed as distance learners

- are highly motivated
- are independent
- are active learners
- have good organizational and time management skills

- have the discipline to study without external reminders
- can adapt to new learning environments

These may sound like the qualities needed to succeed in any learning environment—and indeed, they are. But the distance learning context puts special pressures on learners to be independent and self-disciplined.

If you are considering distance learning, it may be partly because you have multiple responsibilities. Because you are probably already balancing a busy life, you (like other distance learners) need to be strongly motivated and able to structure your world to allow time for studying. *The fact is that you are likely to find that distance learning is more, not less, demanding than learning through traditional means.*

Successful distance learners develop their own support systems, either through electronic gatherings or in person. Chapter 6 of this Guide offers some specific suggestions to help you succeed in a distance learning environment.

EARNING A DEGREE

Is it possible to earn an entire degree without setting foot on a campus? Yes, indeed it is. Chapter 2 provides detailed information about finding a distance education provider or providers offering courses that can lead to a degree.

Undergraduate Degrees. Two-year associate degrees are the fastest-growing segment of distance learning. Public Broadcasting Service's *Going the Distance* program, offered by a consortia of public television stations and community colleges nationwide, now makes available an associate degree for adults who could not otherwise obtain a degree. A number of colleges are offering online associate degrees—either alone or in consortia formed with other colleges in their state.

It is possible to find four-year bachelor's degree programs (B. S. or B. A.) offered at a distance by higher education institutions. Business, liberal arts, and computer science fields are the four-year degrees most often offered via distance learning technologies. There are also several bachelor's degree completion programs, which enable students with associate degrees to complete the remaining requirements for a bachelor's at a distance.

There are several ways you could earn an undergraduate degree as a distance learner:

1. Complete a degree program from a single institution. A few years ago, most colleges and universities offered only a smattering of individual courses to students at a distance, but many institutions now offer degree programs via technology. As a result, you are likely to be able to find a complete program in the field in which you are interested. It may even be offered at a distance by an institution you have always dreamed of attending.

2. Accumulate credits from several institutions. Another way you could achieve a degree from a distance is to accumulate courses and credits from more than one college or university. *Before* embarking on this course, however, be sure that courses and credits you plan to earn from one institution will be accepted toward a degree that you hope to receive from another. Transferring credits is like putting together a picture puzzle: To fit, the pieces must be of the same picture. (This is discussed more fully later.)

3. Prove your competency. A third way to get a degree via distance learning is by enrolling in an institution that bases credentials on proven competencies rather than on earned credit hours. Traditionally, higher education institutions have awarded degrees when a student has accumulated a certain number of credit hours in required subjects. However, distance learning is moving in the direction of a new model, which is based on independent verification of a learner's competency. Under this system, you might obtain formal recognition for your competency through assessments and then enroll in only the courses you need to complete a degree program.

Institutions that use this system (for example, the Western Governors University) do not require you to complete any particular courses or number of hours. Instead, they ask you to demonstrate mastery of subjects through written and other exams. Your degree will be based on your proven competency in a particular field.

Even some conventional institutions, which rely on the course credit system rather than demonstrated competencies, will let you earn credits by "testing out" of a particular course by demonstrating your competency.

Postgraduate Degrees. It is also possible to earn advanced degrees from a distance. Master's degrees are available in a growing number of fields, especially in business, education, nursing, engineering, and computer science. Some of these programs may require at least a short period of on-campus attendance. Ph.D. and professional programs, such as medicine or law, almost always require some time on campus.

Is a Degree Earned via Technology Equal to One Earned on Campus?

You may be skeptical that a degree earned via technology at a distance will be valued as highly as one earned through on-campus study. You may be wondering whether such a degree might be judged inferior when you look for a job or apply to graduate school. The answer to this understandable concern is that both employers and graduate schools now generally consider degrees earned via technology at a distance equivalent to those earned on campus. Most colleges and universities are genuinely committed to ensuring that distance degrees represent the same overall quality as traditional degree programs. At some institutions, your transcript will look identical to that received through on-campus study.

In the past, there has been prejudice against many degrees earned from a distance rather than in the traditional way. Such prejudice still exists among some employers and some graduate schools. However, these attitudes are rapidly changing as colleges and universities strive to create excellent distance learning programs—and as former distance learners demonstrate their worth in the workplace and in top-notch graduate schools.

WHAT ABOUT TAKING A FEW COURSES?

Not a bad idea. There are thousands of courses available, both for credit and noncredit. If you are just beginning to consider pursuing a degree via distance learning, you might want to enroll in a course or two to see how you like distance learning—whether it fits your lifestyle and your learning style. Many people are taking distance learning courses for personal enrichment or just for fun. Noncredit courses may appeal to you for these reasons.

Doctors, nurses, teachers, and those in some other professional fields must take a certain number of hours in continuing education each year, they earn Continuing Education Units (CEUs) this way. Distance learning is becoming increasingly popular as a way to earn CEUs. If you plan to pursue required continuing education through distance education, however, be sure to find out if units, or credits, from the program you are considering will be accepted.

Even if you are already enrolled in a campus-based degree program, there are many reasons you might want to enroll in a few courses at a distance. Why? Some answers are the following:

- You need a specific course to graduate, but all on-campus sections are full or not offered at a convenient time.
- You want to take a course in an area of interest from a noted professor who teaches via distance learning or teaches elsewhere.
- You are interested in a course that isn't offered at your college or university.
- You're in a hurry to graduate and have some free time over the summer.

In short, there are many opportunities for taking a particular course and many valid reasons for doing so.

Will Another College Accept Distance Education Courses?

Sometimes, but you should check in advance. Transferability of credits is determined by individual institutions. It may depend on factors such as whether the institution where you took the credits was accredited and whether the course itself was considered to be academic in nature. If you are enrolled in a degree program at one college and would like to transfer credit hours earned at a distance from another institution, be sure to find out if those courses will fulfill requirements at your "home" institution.

Some institutions have established formal relationships with other colleges; these colleges have mutually agreed to accept each other's courses. In other cases, a two-year college may have developed what are called *articulation agreements,* or guaranteed transfer, with a four-year institution in the same state. Within some state university systems, credits are transferable between institutions.

THE QUALITY QUESTION

The question of distance learning's quality is bound to be important to you. An inferior education will do you no good, no matter what your goals. However, distance learning does match up to traditional classroom approaches.

"No significant difference." This phrase sums up the result of nearly all research studies on whether students studying at a distance perform as well as their counterparts in traditional classrooms. The research to date indicates that students studying at a distance do as well as on-site students on exams and other measures of achievement. Most studies suggest that the instructional format (that is, an instructor in the classroom vs. videotapes, interactive video, or computers at a distance) has little effect on students' achievement.

One recent study confirms this point. In 1996, a California State University, Northridge, professor carried out an experimental design to compare the effects on students' exam performance of face-to-face student–teacher interaction with virtual interaction. The 33 students in a social statistics course were randomly divided into two groups: One was taught in a traditional classroom and the other taught via the World Wide Web.

The distance students scored an average of 20 percent higher than the regular students did on two examinations. In addition, students in the virtual class felt they had more peer contact and spent more time on class work. They also reported they had more flexibility, a better understanding of the material, and a more positive attitude toward the subject than the students in the traditional class.

IS DISTANCE LEARNING FOR YOU?

By now you should have a sense of the types of distance learning. You should be able to imagine some of the ways it can meet various student interests and needs. You may be ready to "flip the coin" or to weigh the pros and cons of whether a distance learning program is for you. Maybe you're on the brink of a decision.

Before you make your decision, consider carefully **what kind of learner** you are and what your **educational** and **professional goals** are. Are you

- serious, self-motivated, and disciplined?
- comfortable with the idea of learning via technology?
- persistent and resourceful in solving problems?

Think again about your goals. Here are some questions to help you consider your own needs:

- What is my educational goal? Do I need to develop some specific skills in the shortest time possible? Do I need a credit course that I can put on my transcript? Do I want to begin a complete degree program? What do I really want?

- Do I have a timetable or a specific date when I need to complete this education?

- Do I want to go to school part time or full time?

- Will I be working part time or full time at the same time? Will my employer reimburse my tuition costs?

- Can I go to a campus or a local learning center (for several meetings in a semester or to access a computer lab) or must the entire educational experience be offered at a distance?

- How do I feel about the educational delivery method? Am I willing to watch videotapes, listen to audiotapes, and interact over the computer?

- Do I have a computer or access to one? Am I willing to buy a computer? (For a discussion of computer requirements, see Chapter 3.)

- How much time can I commit to my course work? When can I do it? Will I have some time at work? Will I find time late at night or early in the morning at home?

- Is cost an important consideration? How much can I afford to spend each month or each semester for tuition and other charges? Do I need to look for an institution that will provide financial assistance?

This list of questions is not comprehensive. It's a starting point. You must determine your needs and then see if available distance learning opportunities can meet them.

You might also want to consider your personal learning preferences to discover more about how you learn best. Some of us learn best through listening, others through active participation, and still others by reading. Most people use a combination of learning styles. If you are interested in finding out what kind of learner you are, ask your nearest college to administer, or refer you to someone who will administer, a learning style test. (You will read more about these learning preferences in Chapter 6.)

CAUTION: LONG-TERM PLANNING AHEAD

If after considering your goals and commitments, you decide that distance learning might meet your needs, you still have a great deal of investigating to do. You will spend a lot of time and money if you enroll in a distance learning program, especially if you intend to earn a degree. It will pay to invest the time it takes to identify your needs clearly and to find a course of study and a reliable institution to help you meet those needs.

BEWARE OF "DIPLOMA MILLS"

Although many excellent institutions offer high-quality distance learning programs, there are a few unscrupulous providers in the business as well. Some "diploma mills" will churn out diplomas without regard for whether they are really earned or not. As long as someone is willing to pay, these "institutions" are willing to grant certification.

The most important way to protect yourself and be sure that you are enrolling in a quality program is to ask the following question: "Is a reputable institution offering this course or program?" Remember that it is easy to put the words "College" or "University" into the title of a business. These terms, suggesting institutional legitimacy, may mean nothing at all.

This is just an early warning signal. Chapter 2 addresses the subject of quality, including accreditation, and it gives you some specific questions you should ask of any institution from which you are considering taking courses.

SUMMARY: YOU'RE ON YOUR WAY!

In this chapter, you've learned the basics about distance learning. You've been introduced to some distance learners and the reasons they have chosen to pursue their educational goals via distance learning. You now know that you must examine your own goals carefully and take stock of whether you believe you have the personal qualities needed to succeed in this new environment. Hopefully, you've also acquired a real sense of what it would be like to enroll in a course or program delivered from a distance. Any questions you might have had about whether distance learning can match the quality of a traditional approach have most likely been answered.

In short, this chapter has shown you how distance learning might offer a route along the information highway toward the education you want. It's up to you to decide if you want to travel further. If you do, the following chapters are your guide for the rest of the way.

CHAPTER 2

CHOOSING A DISTANCE EDUCATION PROVIDER

Asking the Right Questions

In this chapter you will

- ◆ learn various ways to identify providers of distance education
- ◆ become familiar with the academic and student service issues important to your success as a distance learner
- ◆ be given a list of questions to ask each potential distance learning provider

Once you have determined your personal learning or professional development needs, it is time to look for the provider that comes closest to meeting them. Let's begin by determining which institutions to approach first.

At this point, it is important to understand that fully one-quarter of the approximately 3,600 accredited colleges and universities in the United States are offering some distance learning opportunities. These range from institutions that offer only a few courses, such as faculty teaching at remote sites, some correspondence courses, a few courses offered by interactive television, and computer-based courses offered over the Internet, to institutions that offer one or more complete degrees at a distance. How should you go about sorting them out and finding the one that is the best match for you?

PROVIDERS CLOSE TO HOME

You should start by considering the public institutions that are geographically close to you for two reasons: (1) if a nearby institution offers what you want through distance learning, you are likely to find better support services, and (2) the in-state tuition is likely to be less expensive. If there is no program close to your home, look at other public institutions within your state. Again, the services are likely to be more available, and you will be paying in-state tuition.

Next, consider the private institutions in your state. Although they are likely to be more expensive than public ones, the cost for distance learners may not be as much as you might expect.

Each state has an education office that is responsible for collecting and disseminating information about higher education in that state. Check the Guide's Web site for a list of all of the state education offices with responsibility for postsecondary education. Check with your state office and in nearby state offices to determine which institutions have the program you are seeking.

REGIONAL AND NATIONAL PROVIDERS

The third option is to look regionally and nationally. Two types of organizations have information about these distance learning opportunities. One is the regional accrediting association in a multistate area (there are six in the United States), such as the New England Association of Schools and Colleges, Inc. The second is the regional higher education association, such as the Western Interstate Commission for Higher Education or the Southern Regional Education Board.

The regional accrediting associations will be able to provide you with information about which of the distance education institutions are accredited and the regional higher education associations will be able to provide a variety of information about those institutions.

 Because information about each of these organizations is constantly changing, we have provided contact information on our companion Web site.

USING PRINT AND ELECTRONIC SOURCES TO FIND A PROVIDER

A final way to find a provider is to search for the course or program using one of the several print and electronic sources for finding information about distance education opportunities.

The most comprehensive listing of electronic information about institutions offering distance education is found on our Web site.

 The Web addresses for more than 900 institutions providing distance education opportunities are listed by state or, if they are regional or national in scope, by the geographical area they serve.

Peterson's 1998 Guide to Distance Learning Programs[1] lists the courses and programs of more than 800 accredited institutions in the United States and Canada. This reference book is designed to be updated every year or two since the number of institutions entering the distance education marketplace is expanding rapidly each year. Offerings are listed by institutions offering (1) degree and certificate programs and (2) individual courses; an index of institutions by state and Canadian province that offer distance learning is also included. Each institution offering distance learning has a detailed profile that describes the institution, the course delivery sites (e.g., home, high schools, workplace), media used (e.g., television, radio, email), services provided (e.g., library, computer, email, advising, career counseling), credit-earning options, typical costs, registration procedures, and contact information at the institution.

[1] 2nd edition; Princeton, NJ: Peterson's, 1997.

An additional distance education electronic information source is Caso (Cape Software), which lists approximately 2,400 courses and other study resources, some of which are available at no charge. In addition, Caso publishes *The Internet University: College Courses by Computer.*

Various search engines provide information about distance learning. Eric Clearinghouse has an entire section on distance education.

See the companion Web site for additional information about Caso and other online sources.

If you cannot find the exact program that you are looking for through the traditional search channels, it may not be available, *yet.* New programs are being developed and offered on a routine basis. You should contact the Western Governors University (WGU) (see our companion Web site for more information) or one of the regional organizations mentioned previously in this chapter and ask if they are aware of any new programs being developed that would meet your needs. Increasingly, you will find institutions working together to create new degrees that, on their own, they would be unable to offer.

As you complete the task of finding courses or programs that fit your needs, you should have identified several potential provider institutions. The next step is to contact each institution to determine the services they provide for distant students. It is in the area of support services that you are likely to find the greatest differences among institutions.

Questions to Ask Distance Education Providers

Most of our understanding of higher education institutions is based on previous experiences on a college campus where academic and student services are offered through various offices. For the distant learner, these services have to be provided by the institution in a different fashion. There is great variation in the way that institutions have addressed these distance learning support issues.

The next step in choosing a provider is comparing the range of services that each institution offers to distance education students. Students often assume that an institution offering courses or programs at a distance will also provide all of the essential services at a distance. In fact, that is far from true. Many institutions have found it easier to put courses and offer degrees on the Web than to reorganize campus services that are essential for distance learners.

The importance of institutional services for you as a distance learner can't be overemphasized. To be blunt, if the institution has not organized services to support you at a distance, you are likely to spend an enormous amount of time trying to connect to an office or individual at the institution, trying to navigate its various campus-based processes (for example, admissions, registration, financial aid, advising, computer connections, library support, etc.) and trying to handle the logistics of sending and securing academic materials. If the services are not in place, problems will persist throughout your program. To avoid the frustration of enrolling in an institution that is not set up to serve you, be careful to obtain answers to each of the questions we have listed on the following pages. A small amount of your time spent researching the services of institutions will have a terrific payoff as you move smoothly through your program.

There are a number of questions to ask each institution. Although this may appear tedious, you will find that the answer to each question is basically "yes" or "no." To make this part of your research

easier, we have included on our Web site a worksheet that you can print and use to record the responses of each institution to the questions outlined below. This form will make comparing responses between institutions much easier. Remember that you are looking for the institution that has the maximum number of "yes" answers.

General Issues

A Web Site.   An institution involved in distance learning usually will have a first-rate Web site describing the programs and services it offers at a distance. If the institution has been serving students at a distance for more than a year or two, it is likely to have a Web section for "Frequently Asked Questions (FAQs)."

1 Does the institution have a Web site with information about distance learning offerings and services?

Phone Access.   Being a distance learning student means that you are physically removed from the traditional opportunities for face-to-face communication with instructors and campus office personnel, but it should not mean that you are a "lonely, or isolated," learner. It

is important to ensure that you have replaced in-person meetings with other forms of communication. For some purposes, the telephone is going to be your most effective and convenient means of communication. If the institution is in your local calling area, phone access will be easy. If it is a toll call, you need to determine who is going to be paying the long distance charges. You don't want to be paying for long distance calls to a campus because you may avoid making calls in order to save money.

2 Is the institution a local call for you?

3 If your answer to question 2 was "No," does the institution have a toll-free number for distance learners that will allow you to connect with faculty and the various campus offices?

An Orientation Handbook for Distance Learners.   It is enormously helpful if the institution has thought through all of the issues and topics of interest to distance learners and put together relevant policies and procedures in a single document. This will save you time in evaluating the institution's commitment to distance learners.

4 Does the institution have an orientation handbook for distance learners?

Orientation for Distance Students.   Once you have decided to enroll at an institution, you might find it helpful to participate in an orientation for distance students. Such an orientation would normally be offered at a distance. An orientation may provide tips on a variety of ways to make learning at a distance easier. Many orientations feature faculty and current students who have special insight into successful distance learning strategies. If the institution you are considering has an orientation program, be sure to take advantage of it.

5 Does this institution have an orientation for distance learners?

A Single Point of Contact.   One of the major frustrations of distance learners is not being able to contact the appropriate person or office on a campus to answer a question, to process paperwork, or to solve a problem. Those institutions that are designed to serve the distance learner normally will have a single point of contact, such as an Office of Distance (or Distributed) Learning.

6 Does the institution have a designated distance education office?

7 If it does, does this office provide "one-stop" services in the areas of:

>   admissions?
>   registration?
>   financial aid applications?

A Contact Person.   You will need a contact person at the institution to serve as your advisor and advocate. You will have numerous process questions related to your program, and it is important to have the same person you can call on campus each time to answer your questions.

8 Will you be assigned an advisor who will assist you in weaving your way through the institutional requirements and processes?

Accreditation.   Institutions that have achieved regional and professional accreditation have met a set of rigorous educational standards. (As noted earlier, a listing of all of the regional and professional accrediting associations is provided on our Web site.) Accredited institutions are recognized by the U.S. Department of Education and approved to award federal financial aid. In addition, other accredited institutions usually accept their credits in transfer. In selecting your program—all other things being equal—your top priority should be an accredited institution.

9 Is the institution regionally accredited?

10 Is the institution accredited by some other federally recognized agency?

Furthermore, many programs lead to some sort of state or national certification and/or examination (for example, a nursing degree). You want to be sure that the institution has state or professional approval to offer a degree for which you will have to take a professional examination or seek state licensure.

11 Does a professional accrediting association accredit the program in which you are interested?

12 If it does, has that professional association approved the program to be offered at a distance?

13 Does the program in which you are interested need to be certified by the state?

14 Upon graduation, will you be able to take the state examination for certification?

Transfer Credit.   You may want to use credits that you have accumulated at a previous institution in the program you have now selected. You want to make sure that all credits earned elsewhere are transferred before you begin the program.

15 Will this institution accept credits that you have earned previously?

16 If it will, how many?

Transcript and Diploma.   You want to make sure that the transcript and the diploma that you receive from the institution are the same as you would receive if you took the program totally on campus. You do not want a transcript or diploma that identifies your courses or program as different from that on campus in order to ensure that a future employer or others will not interpret the degree as "second-class."

17 Will my transcript and diploma look the same as if I had taken the courses on campus?

Academic Issues

Academic Advisor.   You will have a number of questions about the program in which you plan to enroll. You will want to make sure that you have an academic advisor, usually a faculty member in the program, before enrolling. This could be the same person as the previously mentioned "Contact Person" (see question 8). Having one person with whom you can raise questions and discuss program issues is very important.

18 Will you be assigned an academic advisor?

19 Will the advisor be assigned before you enroll to help you choose courses?

Percentage of the Program at a Distance.   At the outset, you want to know how much of the program is available fully at a distance. If there are any courses, portions of courses, laboratories, discussions, examinations, or other components of the program that will require you to go to the campus or another location, you need to know this in advance. You should inquire about prerequisite courses and any general education requirements that may be necessary before you can begin work in the major. When you inquire about the percentage of the program offered at a distance, make sure that the institution understands that you are asking about every requirement of the program, including internships and externships. Finally, you also will want to know well in advance if any location-specific requirements are scheduled so that you can fit them into your own schedule.

20 Is 100 percent of the program offered at a distance?

21 If not, what percentage of the program is available at a distance?

Residency Requirement. The vast majority of higher education institutions have requirements about the number of credits you must take on the campus, or at an approved off-campus location, in order to complete graduation requirements. This requirement ranges from one-quarter to one-half of the credits needed to graduate. If the institution counts all courses offered by the institution for residency, regardless of where the student is located, then the distance student can meet the requirement. If the requirement specifies some amount of time on campus, this may be a major barrier to your timely completion of the program.

An institution that has recently begun offering degrees at a distance may not have revised all of their own internal campus policies to take into account the realities of distance learners. You must resolve this issue before you enroll in a program. If the program does not have a waiver of the residency requirement for distance students, you need to consider whether you can fit travel to a campus or another site into your schedule.

22 Does the institution have a residency requirement?

23 If yes, can a distance student fulfill the requirement at a distance?

Sequencing of Courses. Most degree programs do not offer all of their courses each semester. Courses in a major are often alternated between fall and spring semesters; and, usually, they are offered only once a year.

Some institutions are admitting a "cohort" of students who begin a program as a group and move through it—usually part time, taking two courses per semester—until they finish together in two to four years. The advantage of the "cohort" system (beyond going through a program with the same group of students, even if virtually) is that the institution guarantees a sequencing of courses, therefore, you know which courses you will be taking each semester of the program. This is important because the sequencing plan has accounted for prerequisites and a logical progression through the program.

You want to be sure that the institution has thought through the sequencing so that all of the courses you need will be offered in the necessary period for you to complete your degree. If a course you need isn't going to be offered during the semester you need it, will you be allowed to take the course from some other institution and have it accepted when transferred?

24 Does the institution have a logical sequencing of courses?

25 If it does, does the institution guarantee the courses will be offered in the sequence listed?

Substituting Courses from Other Institutions.   Although you may never need to exercise this option, it is useful to know if you can take a course from another institution and substitute it for one in your program. If you or a family member were ill for a time, or your job responsibilities changed and you had to withdraw from a course that wouldn't be offered for another year, you would want the option of being able to take the course elsewhere in the summer or a later semester so you do not slow your progress toward the degree.

26 Does the institution allow courses to be substituted from other institutions?

27 If it does, is there a limit?

Placement or Admissions Testing.   If there are any tests that you must take before admission (for example, the Scholastic Aptitude Test or Graduate Record Exam), you should know about them and where they are offered. If you are required to take any placement examinations (for example, math or a foreign language), you should also know about them. Moreover, you should know whether your performance on these tests could affect whether you can take your entire program at a distance.

28 Are there any required examinations that you must take before enrollment?

29 If there are, are they offered at a distance?

30 Could your performance on any examination influence whether you could take your entire program at a distance?

Library Access.   You will read more in Chapter 4 concerning library issues and academic support for the distance learner. Before enrolling, there are a few questions to ask providers to help you decide about their library services.

Libraries are rapidly moving toward providing information and resources electronically. You will be able to complete an enormous amount of research over the Web. However, actually securing library resources can often be one of the most difficult problems for distance learners. If you live in a rural area that does not have a college or university library nearby, you need to consider how your library needs will be met. A reasonable expectation is that the distance learning institution has made some special provisions for providing library materials to distance learners, including interlibrary loan, 48-hour delivery, or faxing services.

At the very least, it is important that the institution have an online library catalog you can access over the Internet so that you can easily determine what is available from the institution. Other questions that you should ask are listed next:

31 Does the library have a toll-free telephone number?

32 Is there a designated librarian for distance students to contact?

33 Is there a "Guide to Library Resources for Distance Students?"

34 Is the library catalog online?

35 Will the library ship books and other materials to distance students?

36 Will the library secure books and other materials from other libraries through interlibrary loan or other means?

37 If it will, does the library pay the fees associated with these services?

38 If it doesn't, what are the costs you will incur for having materials sent to you?

Computer Access. A computer, with Internet access, is rapidly becoming the essential tool for distance learners. You will have a chance to examine this topic in more detail in Chapter 3. Increasingly, distance learning programs require students to have access to a computer in order to connect to the campus by email, to receive and transmit assignments electronically, to access the online library catalog, and for many other purposes. Knowing the institution's expectations about access to a computer by distance learners is an important issue in selecting a provider.

39 Do I need regular access to a computer?

40 Does the institution have clear standards on what computer capabilities I need for my degree program?

41 Will I need access to the Internet?

42 If I will, does the institution provide Internet access for distance learners?

43 Is there a special fee for Internet access?

The Bookstore. You will need textbooks and other materials as you progress through your program. It is certainly most convenient and efficient if the institution provides bookstore services for distance students. If the institution does not provide this service, you should ask about arrangements you will need to make to secure your course materials.

44 Does the institution have bookstore services for distance students?

45 If it does, does the bookstore have a toll-free telephone number?

46 Can books be ordered online over the Internet through a server that will protect your credit card information?

47 If it doesn't, how do distance students secure course materials?

Financial Issues

Tuition. The major expense for any program, in most cases, is the tuition. If you are attending a program in your own state, you probably qualify for in-state tuition. If you are attending an out-of-state public institution, you want to determine if you are eligible for in-state tuition. Some states have set a distance learning rate for all students, regardless of where they live. It is worth exploring this issue with each institution because the in-state tuition rate is often one-third of the out-of-state rate.

48 If you enroll in the state in which you live (as an in-state student), what is the tuition rate?

49 If you enroll as an out-of-state student, what is the tuition rate?

Fees.   For many institutions in recent years, fees, separate from tuition, have become an important source of revenue. There are often special fees assessed for technology (usually referring to computer connections), distance learning support (which pays for shipping materials to students), library fees for distance learners, and student activities (in which distance learning students rarely have an opportunity to participate). When totaled, these fees can be substantial, and they should be factored in when determining the costs of a distance learning experience.

In addition to the fees charged by the institution, you may have a monthly connection fee to an Internet provider (see question 43).

50 Does the institution have fees in addition to tuition?

51 What are the amounts of each fee charged to distance learning students?

Financial Aid.   If you are going to require some level of financial assistance in the form of grants, scholarships, a work-study program, or loans, you want to be sure that the institution makes these forms of assistance available to distance students. In addition, you want to learn if the institution "counts" a distance learning student as equal to an on-campus student for financial aid purposes. Some institutions have chosen to award distance students a reduced percentage of aid compared to a student taking the same load on campus. Their argument is that distance students are living at home and don't have commuting costs, and so, their financial need is less.

The federal government is considering changes in current financial aid regulations that would expand opportunities for distance learners. Check our Web site routinely for updates on this important topic.

52 Does the institution award full financial aid to distance learners?

53 If it doesn't, for what types and level of aid are distance learners eligible?

Student Service Issues

Admission to a Program. If your goal is a certificate or a degree, at some point you will need to seek admission to the program. Many students apply for admission to a program after they have completed several courses in order to validate their original interest in that field of study and their degree of comfort with learning from a distance. Others wish to be admitted before they take any courses so they can ensure that all courses they complete will count toward their degree. In some professional fields, students may not be allowed to take courses until they have been admitted to the program.

If you have completed courses prior to admission, whether at the institution where you are applying or elsewhere, you want to make sure it is considered in the admission process (see the previous discussion on page 30 about transferring credits). Moreover, if you feel that you have acquired prior learning through some nontraditional learning experiences, you should inquire if that can be considered in the admission process or granted after admission.

54 Does the institution give credit for prior learning?

55 Does the institution allow you to "test out" of a course or courses?

56 Can you take courses before being admitted?

57 Will the institution accept transfer credits in your program?

Registration. An increasing number of institutions are developing alternatives to face-to-face course registration, including mail-in, online, and interactive voice response (IVR) telephone registration systems. Online and IVR systems were actually designed to speed up the process for on-campus students, but they also benefit the distance learner. After you have resolved other issues related to attending at a distance, you want to make sure that you don't have to drive to campus to register for courses.

58 Does the institution provide options for me to register at a distance?

Career Counseling. If you are pursuing additional education with the goal of seeking a job, changing jobs, or beginning a career, you will want to find out if career counseling services are available to distance education students. Some campus-based career centers are creating Web sites that list their resources. Many are willing to review drafts of your resume and cover letter electronically and then provide comments.

59 Does the institution provide access to career counseling services for distance learners?

60 Can you receive career counseling services at a distance?

SUMMARY: KNOW WHAT TO EXPECT

The number of issues that have been outlined in this chapter may seem a bit overwhelming. But, they are important issues and you need to secure answers. Too many students—on or off campus— begin a college experience without really knowing what to expect. If you have answers to the questions outlined in this chapter, you shouldn't encounter many surprises during your educational journey.

CHAPTER 3

THE ROLE OF THE COMPUTER IN DISTANCE LEARNING

Succeeding Online

In this chapter you will
- learn how computers are used in distance learning
- determine the kind of computer, accessories, and software you will need
- learn how to upgrade your existing computer or buy a suitable one
- learn how to access and use the Internet

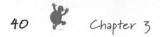

WHY YOU NEED A COMPUTER

As a distance learning student, you will need to use a computer for many different purposes. You will use word-processing and other general-purpose software to prepare assignments and papers. You should also expect to communicate with faculty members and other students, access online information resources, and perhaps use specialized computer programs for class exercises or projects, simulations, and experiments. You need to own or have regular access to a computer to complete Internet-intensive courses.

Many classes that rely on videotape, CD-ROM, or satellite, may use email or the Web as the primary form of communication. For these courses, you don't have to own a computer, but you should have easy access to a computer.

If You Own a Computer

For those who own a computer, this chapter and our Web site will help you find out if your computer will work for online distance learning. If it won't, we'll give you some ideas to help you decide whether to upgrade your current computer or buy a new one. We'll also help you ask the right questions to get the software and peripherals (accessories) you need for your computer.

If You Don't Own a Computer

For those who don't have a computer, perhaps you have been thinking of buying one. It may be to help your children with their homework, to email friends or family, to explore your hobbies and/or interests on the Web, to help organize your finances for home or business, or perhaps even to trace your genealogy. Your educational use is one more justification for the purchase. We'll help you decide what computer to buy and what software and peripherals you'll need. We'll even give you some pointers on how to learn to use it. If you can't afford a computer, we'll give you some strategies about where you might find one that you can use.

If You Are an Experienced Computer User

If you are familiar with using a computer, you will find the first part of the chapter useful in understanding how computers are used for distance learning. The last part of the chapter may be useful for review.

If You Don't Feel Comfortable Using a Computer

If you've never used a computer or have used one very little, you may be concerned about using a computer for learning. Anyone contemplating taking college courses is capable of learning to use the computer. If you don't feel comfortable, take some time now to learn about computers. It will be easier to learn now than when you are under the additional pressure of a class assignment. Additionally, you will have more confidence when you start your program of study and be more informed when purchasing a computer.

Your local library may have minicourses on computer use. Local adult education programs at high schools or community centers are relatively inexpensive and provide a comprehensive introduction. Community colleges and universities offer continuing education courses in a wide range of computer topics. Computer stores often have seminars to introduce customers to their computers or the Web. Bookstores are full of books on computers, and some of the large stores may offer computer courses of their own.

You might want to take an informal route by working with a friend or neighbor who has a high level of computer knowledge. Almost any neighborhood 10-year-old can help you with the basics. Today's children are growing up with computers and can't imagine a world without them. But recognize that your friend or neighborhood 10-year-old may know a lot about computers but be a lousy teacher. If the informal route doesn't work for you, don't despair. It's not your fault! The person just isn't the right teacher for you. In that case, find a course to take and rely on your friend or neighbor to help you with problems. Again, if you want to be successful, make sure you are comfortable with basic computer use before you sign up for a distance learning course.

USING YOUR COMPUTER FOR DISTANCE LEARNING COURSES

What Is the Internet?

The Internet is a global system of networks connecting millions of computers and allowing the sharing of information such as email, Web pages, computer files, audio, and video. Also called the *Net*, personal computers and computers called *servers* are connected by telephone lines, satellite, and other types of telecommunications. All of these telecommunication connections form a "net" around the earth. If one of the connections isn't working, the signals find another route around the connection to assure messages get through.

The Internet was started by the U. S. government in 1969 to link together researchers in different facilities across the country, including colleges and universities. The Internet did not become heavily used until the late 1980s and early 1990s when personal computers were being networked rapidly for email and other applications. The Web came along in the early 1990s, and the Internet became a much easier network to use, leading to its phenomenal growth. The rest, as they say, is history!

Online Course Discussions

- The most common discussion tool in distance learning courses is email, usually using a Listserv. The faculty member or a student either starts a discussion by typing in a message on a new topic or responds to the email that others have sent.

- A computer conference is another form of discussion group. It is organized so that it is easy to follow a topic of discussion from its start to finish. A conference is similar to email, except that the messages in a conference are arranged by topic while most email programs organize the messages by the date and time the message was sent. Each student reads and makes their comments over a set period—from a day to several weeks.

- You may need to use a chat room to "talk" to other students by typing in messages on your computer. The writing appears immediately on each participant's screen. In distance learning, these chat rooms are used for discussions and team, or group, work. Examples include Internet Relay Chat (IRC), multiple user dungeons (MUD), MUD object oriented (MOO), and a variety of Web software.

The Web and Your Courses

The *World Wide Web*, also known as the *Web* or *WWW*, consists of files on millions of computers interconnected by the Internet that allow you to view and hear multimedia—text, pictures, audio, and video.

- You use a software program called a *Web browser* on your personal computer to connect and display information from a Web site computer called a *server.*

- A Web site's address is called a *universal resource locator* (URL), and it usually begins with http://www. or www. with the remainder of the site address following.

- Web pages often have text and images termed *links* that you can click on to view a different Web page on the same server or from a server anywhere in the world.

- Web pages are written in a computer language called *hypertext mark-up language* (HTML).

- For some courses you may need to use Web browser plug-ins that add new functions, such as document delivery, audio, video, and Internet telephone. Java and Active-X are computer languages that many plug-ins use for animation or other advanced features. (See the "Introduction to Using the Web" box for more details.)

Your Course May Use the Web for Many Different Purposes

Course materials and information, such as a syllabus, assignments, exercises, examinations, and class discussions, may be posted to the Web. Increasingly, the Web is used as the primary way to deliver a course. If the course is delivered primarily on the Web, the course Web site will have detailed information to supplement or replace a textbook and extensive links to other Web sites to bring a wealth of information to your learning experiences.

You may take tests on the Web, either an open-book at-home test, or you may be required to come to a testing site where a proctor can ensure the security of the testing. You may also use the Web to discuss materials by exchanging email or by participating in a computer conference or a chat room (see "Online Course Discussion").

Courses on the Web often take full advantage of the possibilities of linking to other pages. For these courses, it is important to understand that the course is not linear like a book. It is similar to searching for materials in a library: Each new Web page leads to more pages as each new source in a library search can lead to another source. There is another similarity in that there are many different authors of Web pages with different perspectives. For some, this lack of continuity and structure is uncomfortable and ambiguous. Don't worry about feeling uncomfortable; you're not alone. For some students, the enjoyment of surfing from one page to another is interesting and stimulating. Don't get lost in following links too far from the faculty member's instructions. If you get lost, you can always go back to your home page by clicking on the "Home" button at the top of the screen or to your course page by clicking on its bookmark.

The Web contains information of all sorts—from factual to unsubstantiated to intentionally incorrect. Some information is ultraconservative and other information is ultraliberal. There are religious sites and pornographic sites. You need to be cautious and evaluate all the information you find on the Web. For more information on researching, see Chapter 4.

Introduction to Using the Web

Following are some simple instructions on using the Web for the first time:

- If you don't have your own computer, find a computer that has access to the Internet and has a Web browser (e.g., Netscape Communicator or Microsoft Internet Explorer) setup on it. (Possible locations for trying a computer include a friend, a college campus, a public library, or high school computer lab.)

- With the computer's mouse, click or double-click on the Web browser icon. The browser will take up to a minute to load.

- Next, you have two choices: You may search for Web sites on different subjects, or you can click on the "Bookmarks" or "Favorites" that are already saved on the computer. Bookmarks and favorites are Web sites that have been filed in the computer's memory during prior use.

- To conduct a search for information, click on the "Search" and follow the onscreen instructions. There are many search sites on the Web, and your browser will have a few bookmarked. To find other Web search sites, do a search using "search engines" as the search words.

(continued)

You can also search by name for some current favorites: Yahoo!, Excite, HotBot, Lycos, Infoseek, Web Crawler, Alta Vista, or Dogpile.

- To call up information from a Web site, you click on the site URL link. (All links to Web pages or sites change the on-screen mouse arrow, or cursor, from an arrow to a hand when you move it over the link.) Text links are usually shown as underlined words or as images. You can determine if there is an active link by moving the cursor over the link and seeing if it changes to a hand symbol.

- You can continue to follow links on each page, or you can click the "Back" button at the top of the screen to back up one page at a time.

- Bookmark the pages you think you will use frequently—while the Web page you want to bookmark is on your computer screen—by selecting "Add Bookmark" or the equivalent command from a menu. This will save it in your computer for future use.

- If you get a Web address (URL) in an email, you can highlight the address, copy it, and then switch to your browser and "paste" it into the "Open Page" address area. This avoids making errors in writing it down and retyping it.

- Both Netscape and Microsoft provide a Web training tutorial. Go to the Guide's Web site for links to their tutorials.

Listservs

Listservs and discussion groups use the Internet to distribute email to groups of people (sometimes thousands of people). Some courses use Listservs to distribute email from one student or the instructor to all the other members of the class. "Discussions" by all the class members and "question-and-answer sessions" between the faculty member or a guest "speaker" and the students are facilitated using Listservs. Most institutions will sign you up for the class's Listserv. If they expect you to subscribe yourself, they will provide directions. Once subscribed, you may send an email to the list address and the Listserv computer will send it out to all subscribers automatically.

Usually, Listservs have an address that you can send commands, such as "subscribe" and "unsubscribe," to. Many people make the mistake of trying to send these commands to the same address to which they send regular email messages. Everyone on the Listserv gets the command intended for the command address, and some will become annoyed at having to open and delete the message. Don't make this mistake! And when someone else makes the mistake, don't send an email about it. It only generates more junk email.

Email and Listserv Tips

All email programs and Listservs have differences, however, all use email messages to communicate. There are some tips that are universal for using them:

- Try to look at each message just once. Read it, and reply if needed. You may keep it, print it, or delete it.

- Many people find it tiring to read long documents on the computer screen, so you may wish to print lengthy information documents for your course. There may be information that you want to keep handy to review or to study in depth. A loose-leaf binder or folder works well for organizing printed pages.

- If you have multiple classes or belong to multiple Listservs, automatically send each to a different folder in your computer, usually called *filtering*, if your mail program supports it. Each email program does this a little differently, so read your email manual or use the help function in your email. Filtering makes it easier to keep each course separate and assures continuity within a folder.

- When you originate a message or reply, try to keep it short (ideally, one computer screen in length). Long messages are hard to read and remember.

- If you have a number of points to make on different subjects, send them out in separate messages over a few days or a week.

- When replying to a message, keep only the relative passage or paragraph of the message that is necessary to keep your comment in context. It is irritating to other students and the instructor when you make them reread the entire original email message before getting to your comments.

- Make sure you participate regularly. The faculty for your course may keep all your email messages and use them for your grade, looking at the quality and number of your postings over the length of the course.

- In email, Internet, and Web courses, everyone can participate in discussions whether by email, Listserv, or computer conferencing. In an on-campus course, those who think fast or like to talk often dominate discussions. In electronic discussions, you can take the time to think about the points you want to make or questions you want to ask, and you can make sure they are phrased the way you want them. Or you can jump in early. Or wait to the end to try to have the last word.

- If you want to make sure your email containing comments, questions, assignments, or papers are received by your faculty member or a Listserv, some of the newer email programs allow you to request an email confirmation. You can request that a confirmation be sent when your instructor's computer or the Listserv computer receives it. A confirmation can also be sent when the faculty member reads it. Before you rely on this method, however, make sure your instructor's email program will provide confirmations. Note that Listservs do not return confirmations from individual subscribers.

- Email is informal. Occasional misspellings and lapses in grammar are tolerated on the Internet. In a class, however, you will probably be held to higher standards. For classes, use standard business letter formatting, skip a line between paragraphs, and use proper grammar, punctuation, and sentence structure.

Email and WWW Addresses Explained

An email address consists of a minimum of five parts.

1. the person's computer name, or user name
2. the symbol @
3. the organization's name, or second-level domain name
4. a period, separating domain names
5. the purpose of the organization, or top-level domain name

(continued)

For example, student Amy Smith, taking courses from Ivy League University in the United States, might have this address:

asmith@ivyu.edu

where asmith is Amy Smith's user name, @ separates the user name from the domain names, ivyu is the second-level domain name of Ivy League University, and edu is the top-level domain name.

There can be third-level domain names, too, such as:

asmith@college.ivyu.edu

where "college" is the third-domain name; note that a period separates it from the second-level domain name.

Web addresses take a similar form usually consisting of at least three parts:

1. www followed by a period
2. the organization's second-level domain name followed by a period
3. the purpose of the organization, or first-level domain name

Ivy League University might have the following main Web page name:

www.ivyl.edu

(The http:// you often find in front of the Web address is not actually part of the address, and with most current Web browsers it is not necessary for you to type it.)

Examples of first-level domain names and their affiliations are

- edu—<u>edu</u>cational, colleges and universities
- com—<u>com</u>mercial, for-profit businesses
- org—<u>org</u>anization, a nonprofit organization
- gov—<u>gov</u>ernment, United States
- mil—<u>mil</u>itary, United States
- fr—<u>Fr</u>ance

(There are many other international notifications.)

Netiquette

Netiquette is a contraction of Inter*net* and et*iquette.* Netiquette describes the things you should or shouldn't do if you want to get along with other Inter*net* citi*zens,* or *netizens.* For example:

- Do not use profanity or make negative or hurtful comments about other students' comments or work. This is called *flaming.* If you are angry or frustrated when you write your email, hold it until the next day, if possible, and always edit your email to remove any negative language or tone.
- In Internet culture, WRITING IN ALL CAPS TELLS OTHERS THAT YOU ARE ANGRY OR EMPHATICALLY MAKING A POINT. Don't do it unless you need to make a point, and *never* use all caps when communicating with your instructors.

There are many other Internet culture issues that you may want to know about. Just put the word "netiquette" in a Web search engine and read about them in the Web links provided.

Internet Discussion Groups

Internet discussion groups, also known as Usenet Newsgroups, are a little different from Listservs. You don't need to subscribe to a discussion group to read the postings. Instead, you use a "newsreader." The Netscape and Microsoft browsers have a newsreader as part of their software. The newsreader accesses a host computer that is running a "newsserver," which is usually provided by your Internet service provider. This allows you to view the most recent messages posted to the discussion group you are interested in. Newsgroups do not require you to sign up to post to the group, but some are moderated and screen postings to prevent "spam," or objectionable material. Before you post to a newsgroup, it's a good idea to just read messages for awhile, known as "lurking," until you understand the culture and scope of the group. It is a breach of netiquette to post messages that are not appropriate to a group's subject.

For use in your course work, you may want to post a question to a discussion group to get some expert information. There are members who are experts who can provide excellent information. There also are those with less subject knowledge than you who are more than happy to play the expert. Some of the most popular categories of discussion groups, known as hierarchies, are:

Alt   Alternative and controversial, including topics such as sex

Biz   Business

Comp Computers and related discussions

Gov   Government

Misc Miscellaneous discussions that don't fit into the other hierarchies

News News about Internet discussion groups, including FAQs and use information

Rec   Arts, hobbies, sports, and recreation

Sci   Scientific topics

Soc   Social issues and socializing

Talk   Debates and other discussions

Within each category, or hierarchy, there are numerous discussion groups (currently more than 20,000) with discussions occurring and information being exchanged from around the world.

Multimedia on Your Computer

Multimedia means more than one medium. In addition to the standard computer display, multimedia includes audio and video. Currently, phone lines have the capacity to carry acceptable quality audio along with the other computer signals on a modem connection. For instructional purposes, the video currently available over telephone lines is suitable for some limited purposes. Reasonable quality motion video should be available over the Internet within the next few years; but for now, it's limited to CD-ROMs.

Audio. Audio includes playing back prerecorded sound on your computer. Examples of educational uses of prerecorded audio include the faculty member's lecturing, guest speakers, presentations, and sounds that illustrate important points in instruction, such as musical phrases for a music appreciation course, speech impediments for a speech therapy class, or announcer styles for a television production class. In some courses, you may be asked to record a speech, for example, for a foreign language course or a television production class, or you may be asked to annotate a text report for clarity. Internet telephone allows multiple students to have simultaneous course discussions among themselves or work on group projects. The faculty member can lead a discussion or review session.

Video.   Video capability can provide recorded video programs that supplement the course materials, lectures by well-known authorities, or add film or television clips. Recorded video can be played from a CD-ROM in your computer or over the Internet if your modem connection is "fast." If the students and faculty member have cameras on their computers, called desktop video, all the students and the faculty member can see each other while they discuss course issues. Video over the Internet is cumbersome right now, but new methods and faster connections will make it commonplace soon.

Many Windows personal computers (PCs) and all Macintosh computers are already equipped for multimedia. Some inexpensive or older computers will need a multimedia kit, consisting of a sound card that goes inside your computer, a CD-ROM (internal—inside your computer or external—a separate box), and computer speakers.

Submitting Your Assignments by Computer

Some distance learning providers will have you mail assignments to them. A much faster way for your work to get to your instructor, and for your graded work to get back to you, is to use a computer. Email, using plain text and attachments, fax, posting to the Web, and File Transfer Protocol (FTP) are four methods. Your instructors will tell you which methods you may use in each course. It's a good idea to send a test message far in advance of the due date of the assignment if it's the first time that you've attempted these methods of submission.

The basic way to email your work to your faculty member is to write the assignment or paper as a regular email. However, some email programs do not have good word-processing capabilities, such as an easy way to cut and paste text, and spelling and grammar checkers, so you may wish to write your assignment in your word processor and copy the text over to an email screen. To do this— while in your word processor—highlight all the text you want to send and use the copy command to copy it to your computer's memory. Then go to your email program and address a new email message to your faculty member. Then use the paste function to place the copied text in the message. Check to see that it all copied; then send it. Word-processed documents lose all their formatting, such as tabs, bold, and underlining, when you use this method. Spreadsheets and databases cannot be sent this way.

Email attachments, also called enclosures, are becoming the preferred way to send text, and they can be used to send spreadsheets and databases. In order to use email attachments, both your email and the instructor's email must be capable of using attachments, and your instructor has to have the same software (e.g., word processor) you used to create the document. The easiest way to tell if your email program can send attachments is to click on "Help," click on "Search," and type in "Attachment" or "Enclosure." Your email program should display the directions on how to attach a file. Before sending your work, complete it in the word processor, spreadsheet, database, or specialized program, and save the file. Remember, or write down, the filename. Then go to your email program and start a new email message to your faculty member. Click the mouse on the "Message Space" and, depending on your email, either use the insert or the file attachment capabilities of your software to attach your document to the message.

You may choose to use a fax modem to send documents directly from the computer without printing them out. When your document is ready to send, you change your printer selection in your print menu to your fax modem. When you print, it prints to the modem; the modem will walk you through how to fax it. Make sure you have your faculty member's fax number on hand when you start this process.

An older method of exchanging files is FTP. Some distance learning programs use FTP for student assignments and papers. When using FTP, complete your work and save the file. Remember the filename. Then you start the FTP program and follow the instructions to send the file. The instructor will give you an address that sends your work to a directory or, perhaps, a Web page. If you don't have an FTP program, you may download one from the Internet. Using FTP may require some help from your distance learning provider's help desk or from the faculty member.

WHAT KIND OF COMPUTER IS REQUIRED FOR COLLEGE COURSES?

What kind of computer will you need? Often, this information is available in the educational institution's printed marketing materials. If you have access to a computer connected to the Internet, look at the distance learning institution's Web page for computer information. If they don't list the computer requirements, they should provide an email address where you can ask more questions. You may prefer to call and ask the institutions you're considering what the minimum and preferred computer specifications are for the class or the degree program in which you are interested. (A toll-free phone number indicates they are likely to be "student-friendly.") The responses you get from these questions may help you to decide whether to take courses from the institution. If they can't answer the questions, don't respond promptly, or don't respond at all, it may indicate that their courses aren't student-friendly either.

Another way to decide what kind of computer you'll need is to find out what software you will use in your courses and use that information to evaluate your options. Most software lists on the outside of the box what minimum computer capabilities are needed for the software to run. You'll want to buy or upgrade to a higher level than the minimum. This will ensure that the software runs quickly and smoothly from the beginning and will allow new versions of the same software to run smoothly, because new versions usually require more computing power to run at the same speed.

Questions to Ask Distance Education Providers

 (Visit the Guide's Web site for a succinct checklist of questions to ask.)

Operating System.   Every computer has an operating system that allows all the applications software, such as word processors and spreadsheets, to work. Most PCs use a version of Microsoft Windows or Apple Macintosh OS (Mac OS). When you decide to buy a computer, your decision about which operating system to buy is decided for you. If you buy a Windows PC, you will be using a version of Microsoft Windows, and if you buy a Macintosh, you will be using a version of Mac OS. There are about ten times the numbers of Windows computers as there are Macintosh computers.

1   What version of Microsoft Windows or Apple Macintosh operating system do you recommend?

Processor Speed.   The processor, also known as the microprocessor or central processing unit (CPU), is the "brain" of the computer. A fast processor allows programs or files to load in your computer faster and saves you "wait time." New versions of software usually require a faster processor to load and operate at the same speed as the old ver-

sion. The higher the number of a processor, the faster it is. Processor speed is usually stated as megahertz (MHz), such as 300 MHz. Two types of processors are Pentium and Power PC.

2 What is the minimum and preferred processor type and speed?

RAM. The memory in a computer is called random access memory (RAM). This memory is where the operating system, software, and the data you type in are stored while you are using the computer. Information in RAM goes away when you turn off your computer or lose power. More RAM allows your computer to work faster, and your waiting time is reduced. RAM size is stated as megabytes (MB), such as 32 MB or 64 MB.

3 What is the minimum memory capacity, or RAM?

Hard Disk Space. When you turn off your computer, the information, such as the operating system, software programs, and your data files (e.g., papers and assignments), are stored on the hard disk for later use. Hard disk capacity is usually stated in gigabytes (GB). When you ask your distance learning provider how much disk space is needed for your class, you're not asking what the overall size of the disk drive you'll need should be. You are asking how much more space the required programs need (if you don't already have them on your computer), plus the space needed for data files.

4 How much, if any, hard disk space is required?

CD-ROM. Some distance learning programs use a CD-ROM for course materials. For motion video, a high-speed CD-ROM drive is needed.

5 Is a CD-ROM needed? If yes, what speed is required?

Modem Speed. The modem allows you to connect with other computers, usually via the Internet, using a telephone line. The faster the modem, the less time you'll wait for information to transfer between your computer and another. Modem speed is usually stated as kilobits per second (Kbps), the larger the number the better. Be sure that your Internet provider can support the top speed of the modem you have.

6 What is the minimum and preferred speed of modem?

Multimedia Requirements. Multimedia accessories, or peripherals, combine on-screen computer images with sound and/or video.

7 Do the courses require the capability to display multimedia?

Sound Card. If sound is part of the instructional materials, you will need the equipment to hear it.

8 Do I need a sound card and speakers?

Microphone/Video Camera. Some courses may require you to participate in discussions over the Internet. These discussions may be just voice, similar to the telephone, or include video so that you may both see and hear the other members of your class.

9 Do I need a microphone or video camera?

Internet Access. In order to access the Web or exchange email you will need Internet access via a modem.

10 Do you provide access to the Internet through local or toll-free numbers?

11 If not, do you have discounts with any Internet Service Providers (ISPs)?

Computer Access. If you know you will need to purchase a computer, the easiest way may be to buy it through a special program sometimes offered by the provider. You get exactly what you need with a minimum of stress.

12 Do you have any special programs through which I can purchase or lease a computer?

Software Requirements. Software, or computer programs, have specific functions, such as for typing papers and assignments (word processor), accessing multimedia on the Internet (Web browser), or mathematical or financial calculations (spreadsheets).

13 What software do you require?

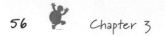
Some distance learning providers require specialized software. You will need to know where and how to get the software. Some providers may send it to you on a disk or CD, you may have to buy it from a bookstore, or you may need to download it from the Internet.

14 Is there specialized course software? If yes, how do I get it? Is it available for the Macintosh computer?

Assignment Submission. Most courses require the submission of assignments or papers. As discussed earlier, there are a number of options for submitting assignments.

15 How will I turn in assignments?

Computer Longevity. Since most degrees take at least two years to complete, and much longer if you're going to school part time, it is helpful to know how long the computer that meets today's needs will last.

16 How many years will the minimum and preferred computer configurations you recommend be capable of being used for your courses?

If the acceptable use period of the computer is less than the time it will take you to complete the courses or degree you desire, factor part of the cost of a computer upgrade or replacement in the cost of the instruction. Also, remember that you use or will use your computer for other lifestyle purposes, so don't think of the total cost wholly for your studies.

Remember that if you are working on a degree with one institution, you may eventually complete it with another. Check the computer requirements of more than one college or university. And remember that the Web has only been in use for a few years, so requirements may change from semester to semester.

 In general, you will use the information above and on the checklist (see our Web site) to evaluate your current computer or purchase a new computer. Specifically, minimum recommendations should be used to evaluate your current computer to determine whether it is suitable, needs to be upgraded, or needs to be replaced. Preferred recommendations should be used to buy a new computer (see the section, "Purchasing a New Computer").

Deciding Whether to Upgrade or Buy a New Computer

Evaluating whether to upgrade a computer or buy a new one is complex. Some say you should never upgrade a computer because computer technology advances so fast that inexpensive upgrades never bring your computer up to current standards. But for distance learning purposes, the issues are a little more concrete. If all you need is a little more memory or RAM, for example, increasing from 16 MB to 32 MB, it is worthwhile to upgrade. If you're handy with a screwdriver, with a little assistance from the supplier you should be able to install it yourself. If you don't want to install an upgrade, have a local computer shop do it for you. Similarly, adding a modem, a CD-ROM drive, a sound card/speakers, or a microphone is easy and worth the trouble. But if you have to add them all, and you have an older computer with a relatively slow processor speed, it probably would be better to buy a new computer.

If you need to upgrade the processor, hard drive, or as noted above, a lot of peripherals, you should purchase a new computer. If your monitor still works well and has a good picture, you should be able to use it with a new computer. If you want to give the old computer to a child, parent, or a friend, then you may want to buy a new monitor.

What's In Your Current Computer?

Once you know what minimum and preferred hardware your distance learning provider recommends, find out what's inside your current computer. The easiest way is to look at an original receipt, or a bill of sale, to see if it provides the necessary information. You can check your instruction manual to see how to look in your computer system's files to see what processor you have, how much RAM you have, and what hardware components are there. The easiest way to figure out what you have is to consult a store that advertises service or upgrades for computers that use your operating system (Windows or Mac). Explain the requirements you have from your distance learning provider and ask them to help you figure out what it will cost to upgrade your computer to meet the requirements. In some cases they may ask you to bring the computer in, but try to get them (or try another store) to talk you through the process on the phone. Once they get you to drag the computer to their store, you are more likely

to let them do the upgrade or let them sell you a new computer. If you do take it to the store, don't let them hurry you into a purchase. Don't end your conversation with the salesperson before you write down the costs for different options. Ask for separate prices for each component so that you can compare prices with other stores.

SHOPPING FOR COMPUTING EQUIPMENT AND SOFTWARE

Do your homework before shopping. Read computer and consumer magazines for reviews of computer equipment and software. Only read reviews for the last three months because computers change so fast. Before shopping for a computer, answer the following questions using the information you receive from your distance learning institution.

Checklist for Purchasing a New Computer
(Visit the Guide's Web site for these questions.)

☑ **Windows or Mac Operating System?** If your distance learning provider does not indicate a preference of operating system (OS), a Windows system may make the most sense. Currently, Windows computers account for over 90 percent of sales, while Mac computers have less than 10 percent of the market. Macintosh computers have integrated hardware and software, so they are often easier to set up and maintain, but fewer stores understand and can support a Mac. However, Macs are prevalent in the arts and education career fields. Windows OS is dominant in the other areas. Most popular programs are available for both.

☑ **Desktop or Notebook?** First, think about whether you want a desktop computer or a notebook, sometimes called a laptop, computer that you can take with you no matter where you go. A notebook allows you to work anytime and anyplace without being tied to a desk. If you travel frequently or will study most of the time away from home, a notebook may be best for you. The desktop computer is less expensive and the screen is larger and easier to read. The full size mouse is easier to use and the keyboard is more comfortable for long-term use. If you think you might want to buy a notebook, keep in mind that to access the Web or your email you must have a phone line available at locations away from home. Most hotel rooms now have computer jacks or phone lines compatible with a modem, and airports have phones with data jacks that work with a modem, but most other locations may prove difficult. Many businesses have digital phone lines that modems cannot use. Accessories for notebooks are more expensive and notebooks are more prone to damage and theft. Batteries are expensive, don't last very long, and plugging into the wall for power defeats some of the purposes of having a notebook. If you have a few hundred dollars extra you can buy a desktop monitor and full-size keyboard and mouse for your notebook and have both capabilities.

☑ **Screen Size?** If you opt for a desktop computer, the size of the monitor you buy is important. A 14 or 15 inch is acceptable; a 17-inch monitor is better. Larger screen size on a notebook is desirable, but it often costs considerably more. If you opt for a notebook, active matrix screens are brighter and less tiring, but they are also more expensive than passive matrix screens. A 12-inch screen is moderately priced, while a 14-inch one adds hundreds of dollars to the cost of a notebook.

☑ **Buy from the Campus?** Some distance learning institutions sell computers; others have relationships with mail-order brand-name companies like Dell and Gateway. Buying a computer this way is easy because the exact computer needed for your courses is specified, and you'll get a reasonable price.

☑ **Brand Name or Generic?** Brand-name computers are more expensive than generic or clone computers. Computers are all made of the same components: case, power supply, motherboard (the heart of the computer), hard disk drive (storage inside your computer for programs and your files), a 3.5-inch floppy disk drive (that uses computer disks that allow you to carry files from your computer to another), CD-ROM, modem, and other peripherals. These components are readily available, interchangeable, and are used to build both brand-name and generic computers. Most brand-name computers are built at a factory, while local stores build most generic computers. If quality components are used, any computer should work well and last for its technological lifetime of two to five years. Technical support for brand-name computers is always available, at some price. Technical

support for generic computers depends on the stability of the company from which you buy it, many are "here today and gone tomorrow." If you do not already know about computers or are not prepared to learn a lot about computers, generic computers are risky.

☑ **Buying Used?**   Used computers are frequently available, but for the most part should be avoided. The classified ads are full of computers that individuals want to sell, but the prices are almost always too high for a computer that is usually obsolete or very nearly so. Or, even worse, the computer may be stolen. Stay away from individuals selling computers unless you know them. Stores may occasionally sell used or refurbished computers, but these are risky because they may be "lemons" returned by other customers.

☑ **Buy Local?**   Local computer stores can provide both brand-name and generic computers, but the brand-name computers are usually more expensive. Locally owned stores will sometimes sell a computer at less than the posted price if you negotiate. The advantage of going to a local computer store is support. Most of the employees will be knowledgeable and helpful. Any seller should repair your computer under warranty, but the local store may be willing to help you set up your computer, help you with any problems you may have, and provide training.

☑ **Buy from a Discount Store?**   Local discount stores provide brand-name computers at reasonable cost. However, the employees often are not knowledgeable, and after-sale support is usually not available.

☑ **Buy from a Mail-Order Company?**   The cheapest price for a given computer will be from a mail-order company. Don't expect much help on the telephone. Generally, you must know exactly what you need to be successful in purchasing from these companies. After-sale support generally is not available. The exceptions are the large mail-order firms like Dell and Gateway, who generally have good customer support before the sale and after, but you pay more than from a smaller company that just sells computers in a box without the additional services.

☑ **Computer Monitors Included?**   Computer monitors seldom are included in the price of the computer. You can buy your computer from one dealer and the monitor from another without concern about compatibility. Some stores sell packages that include the monitor and a printer, and these packages may be a good value. Sometimes stores will sell a computer at a low price, knowing that they will make a profit on the monitor. "Price shop" and carefully evaluate both package and individual component costs.

☑ **Which Modem?**   The faster the modem the better, but a fast modem will not help you if your ISP has a slow modem. If you buy a fast modem, eventually the ISP will upgrade their modem speed and your modem will work at the new, faster rate. If you are buying a new computer, get one already installed inside (internal) your computer. If you are buying a modem for an existing computer, you have a choice of an internal or external one. An external modem is a "box" that plugs into a serial port on your computer and into an electric outlet. If you need to send or receive faxes for your classes, make sure to get a fax modem. The fax modem will allow you to send files from your computer. Unless you buy a scanner, you will not be able to fax originals, such as handwritten notes, drawings, and the like, that are not a file on your computer. There are two other options. You may choose to buy a fax machine or use a local copy center to fax at a per-page rate. If your faculty member will be faxing your graded work back, you should either leave your computer or fax machine on all the time to receive the fax or arrange to be called before a fax is sent. Neither option is ideal; you could also consider having your work faxed back to a local copy center or other business if possible.

☑ **Buying a Printer?**   If you need or want a printer, shop for it separately. As noted above, you will find stores with package prices that include the printer, but you should price the separate components to ensure you're paying the lowest price for the printer you want. You will need to decide between a laser (black) printer or an ink-jet (black and color) printer. The least expensive printer is an ink-jet printer, but the cost per page is usually less for laser printers. The most inexpensive printer will suit your needs for your classes, but your other uses of the computer may convince you to buy a more expensive printer. Printers that are more expensive provide higher resolution, or sharper characters, and print faster, reducing the time you wait for lengthy documents to print than less expensive models. Printer features, quality, and costs are improving rapidly, so do some Web research on the latest before purchasing.

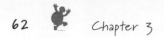

☑ **What Accessories (Peripherals) Do You Need?**　Some distance learning programs may require additional peripherals, such as a microphone to record your voice or to discuss issues over the Internet (like a phone call). Increasingly, courses use cameras that you place on top of your computer monitor to videoconference with the other students and faculty in your class.

☑ **Paper or Plastic?**　Always pay by credit card for computer purchases (or for any costly items) because the credit card provider gives you some extra protection and help if something goes wrong with the deal or the computer.

WHAT SOFTWARE WILL YOU NEED?

At a minimum, you'll probably need the following essential software (but see your checklist for distance learning provider's requirements):

☑ a word processor to write papers, reports, letters, and other documents

☑ a Web browser to access the Web sites on the Internet

☑ an email package, if you're not going to use the email function in the Web browser

You also may need:

☑ a presentation program for organizing and presenting class projects and reports

☑ a spreadsheet program to work with numbers and budgets

☑ a database program to organize data for projects or research

☑ plug-ins, or small programs, that bring new capabilities to your Web browser

☑ specialized software required by the distance learning institution

Software suites combine programs for word processing, spreadsheets, databases, and presentations into a single package, and they are more economical if you need most of the programs listed above. In addition, most Web browsers, and some email

packages, are available at no cost on the Web if you are using them for academic purposes. Check the Guide's Web site for the current Web addresses to download browsers and email packages.

Can't Afford a Computer?

If you can't buy a computer at this time but want to take a class, check into using a friend's computer or the library's public access computers. If you work for an employer that has computers connected to the Internet, ask to use a computer after regular work hours. If you are planning to be a full-time student, the distance learning institution may be able to provide a scholarship or other financial aid to help you buy a computer. Many campus credit unions have special low rates for computer purchases. Many mail-order companies now provide lease/purchase options with monthly payments. At the end of the lease you either pay a small amount to keep the computer or get a new computer and continue your payments.

SELECTING AN INTERNET SERVICE PROVIDER

Checklist for Selecting an Internet Service Provider (ISP)

(Visit the Guide's Web site for helpful questions to ask the ISP.)

☑ Some distance learning institutions have toll-free numbers to a modem pool that you can access at no cost. If so, you can dial in to connect with the campus and the Internet and/or Web.

☑ If your campus doesn't have a local or toll-free modem pool you'll need a company—an ISP—that connects you to the Internet and the Web, either through a modem on a phone line or a connection via cable television. If your distance learning institution doesn't have a discount arranged with an ISP, ask friends what ISP they use or check your Yellow Pages under Internet or computers for ISP listings.

☑ Choose an ISP that provides high-speed (28.8, 33.6, 56 Kbps, or greater) connections to the Internet. If your modem can support the highest speed offered, you'll spend less time waiting for information to transfer to you.

☑ An ISP may charge for connect time in two ways. One is unlimited connect time for a monthly flat fee. The second is a flat charge for a number of hours, with additional cost for extra hours. The institution that you're taking your courses from should be able to tell you approximately how many hours per week you will need for a given course. Remember, too, that you probably will use the Web for more than course work, so plan accordingly.

☑ Avoid ISPs that cut costs by keeping the number of phone lines for you to dial into too low. This results in frequent busy signals, especially during the more popular evening and weekend times.

☑ If you own a notebook and travel overnight frequently, you may want to pick a national or international ISP, so that you can dial in without long-distance charges from your hotel.

☑ There are national providers, like America On-Line (AOL), CompuServe, and Microsoft Network (MSN), that provide access to the Internet along with their own services, such as databases, email, and chat rooms. The additional services are usually more expensive and are not necessary for your distance learning courses. These providers have, at times, grown so fast they have not been able to keep up with user demand, resulting in frequent busy signals for subscribers. These fast-growth pains are also experienced by some local ISPs.

☑ Cable television companies are beginning to provide Internet access that has a much higher speed than telephone ISPs. If the total cost of the service is close to the same cost as a telephone ISP in your area, and if you can afford it, it's worth a little more for the added speed.

☑ A good ISP should have readily accessible technical support at the times you will be working. Technical support available 24 hours a day, 7 days a week (24 by 7) is best, especially if your connection dies in the middle of writing that last-minute paper.

☑ Most Internet access providers provide an email account as part of the service. If you have additional family members that use your computer, ask the ISP if they will provide free email accounts for them.

☑ If you have an Apple Macintosh computer, make sure the ISP's technical support staff is familiar with them.

When you sign up for an ISP, they will give you a user name and password. They should also provide you with computer programs to connect to them, a Web browser, and a "mailbox" for email. Some will provide you with a Web home page that you can use to provide information to others about you, your interests, or expertise. When you register for a distance learning class, the distance learning institution may give you a user name and password as well.

Amy Goes to Ivy League University . . .
and Stays at Home

Amy is a single mother of two who wants to improve her job skills. She decided that she is going to seek a degree at Ivy League University. She chose Ivy League over several others because of its reputation and affordable cost after financial aid and because they seemed to be student-friendly. She won't have to go to a campus every week, and with two children, that's important to her.

Ivy League recommended she buy a copy of *The Distance Learner's Guide*. After reading it, Amy went to her local library to use the Web. With the help of her six-year-old daughter, Maggie, she went to the Guide's Web site and looked at up-to-the-minute information about resources available to her.

WEB

Since she hasn't used a computer much and doesn't own one, she printed out a copy of the computer-related checklists on the Web site: "Questions to Ask Distance Education Providers," "Purchasing a New Computer," and "Selecting an Internet Service Provider (ISP)." First she called up Ivy League and asked them the questions on the "Questions to Ask Distance Education Providers." She found out that she needs the following minimum computer equipment: a Windows 95 computer with a 233 MHz processor, 32 MB of RAM memory, and about 100 MB of free hard disk space. Since she plans to get a new computer, she knows she'll have plenty of hard disk space. The computer she plans to buy will also need a 16X CD-ROM drive, a 28.8 Kbps fax modem, Microsoft Office 97 software suite (Word word processor, Excel spreadsheet, Access database, and PowerPoint presentation software), Eudora email, Netscape Communicator or Microsoft Explorer Web browser, with Adobe Acrobat document software, and Real Audio browser plug-in. Ivy League will send a CD-ROM disk with video segments for one of her classes. Ivy League has arranged for discounted ISP access, but recommended that she shop around to see if she can find a less expensive option. She will turn in her assignments and papers in the way specified by each of her instructors, either faxing them directly from her computer or as email attachments. They were not willing to commit to how long the computer would be suitable for her, but thought "at least two years." Ivy League said that she could buy exactly the computer she wants from their computer store on campus.

(continued)

Since her finances are tight, Amy uses the information she received from Ivy League, along with information from reading this chapter, to call the campus computer store and a couple of local computer stores, one a large computer chain and the other locally owned. She filled out a separate checklist for each. She decided to buy from the campus store because the cost was about the same, and she felt they would provide the best service. Amy purchased the minimum recommended computer, but added a computer printer so she could print out long course messages and her children could use it to print out school projects.

While she was waiting to receive her computer, she talked with her good friends, Carole and Iris, who have computers hooked to the Internet. Both friends agreed that there are several good local ISPs, but they are both paying more than Ivy League's discounted national Internet provider charges. She called the national provider and arranged for service. They told her that they would send a disk to set up her computer for their service.

Amy enrolled in an introductory class on the Internet and the Web at her local high school. They were offering them once a month, and the woman at the school said that Amy was lucky to get into the class. The classes are always full, but they just had a cancellation.

Her computer arrived a few days later, and she asked Russ, a friend, to help set it up. She was surprised how easy it was—the cables would only fit one way. Even her 11-year-old son, Matt, helped—just like when they got their new computer at school. Everything worked—as it should.

She was not so lucky with the Internet access. Amy set up her computer software with the disk the ISP had sent her, but it didn't work. Although it was 10 P.M.—she didn't have time until the children were asleep—the ISP's technical support number was answered after a five-minute wait, and they walked her through the setup. She had to hang up to test the setup because she couldn't afford a second telephone line for her computer. It worked!

The first thing Amy did was go to the Web site for her first course. There was a message from the faculty member welcoming the class and telling all the class to check their email. When she checked, she had email from two of her faculty members welcoming her again and asking that she respond with a short paragraph about herself.

The next day, Amy tells her friend Marcia, "I wasn't sure I could do this, but now I know I can do it. I've been out of school for a long time. Even the computer seemed scary at first, but it's much easier than I thought."

ARE YOU READY FOR ONLINE COURSES?

The final test to see if you're ready for your online class: Connect to the Guide's Distance Learner Web site. You'll find updated information, especially on constantly changing parts of the book, such as this computer chapter. Happy Web surfing!

Summary: Questions to Ask Distance Education Providers

1. How many hours per week will I need to use a computer?
2. How many hours per week will I need to be connected to the Internet?
3. What kind of computer will I need?
4. How many years will I be able to use the computer you recommend for your distance learning courses?
5. What peripherals and accessories do I need?
6. What software will I need?
7. Do you have recommendations about where to buy my computer, accessories, or software?
8. Do you provide Internet access, or have a discount plan with an Internet Service Provider?
9. Is financial aid available to help pay for computer related costs?
10. What kind of technical support do you provide? Telephone, fax, email, or Web support? What hours is support available?

CHAPTER 4

THE DISTANCE LEARNER'S LIBRARY

The Indispensable Guide to Finding the Material

In this chapter you will

◆ learn about the online library catalog

◆ become familiar with interlibrary loans

◆ discover your options in securing learning materials

◆ find out how to use the Internet and the World Wide Web to secure learning materials

From ancient times, the library has been a special place. The manuscripts, scrolls, tablets, and books containing the world's knowledge and ideas were housed there. If scholars needed access to the recorded information and ideas of the day, they spent a lot of time in the library's reading room.

The typical reading room is still a busy place, but the library itself is a much different institution. The ancient library stood alone, collecting—and carefully protecting—the books and documents in its possession. The modern library is part of an international network, exchanging material with others, and with much of its information online.

In most libraries the traditional card catalog has disappeared, having been replaced by more accurate and timely online computer catalogs. Many journals, newspaper files, and government publications are no longer limited to the collection inside the library walls, but are instantly available online. Local and national database services offer you the option of downloading or emailing articles and documents to your computer or receiving them by fax.

Forget the stereotype of the stuffy library housing stern librarians whose mission seemed to be to keep everybody quiet and on task. Today's library is a major key to the information age, and today's librarians may be the distance learner's best friends.

Still, not every library can be equally responsive, not every online source is equally authoritative, and some services can cost you money that you need not spend. This chapter will brief you on what modern libraries and information sources can do, and will explain why some of them can serve you better than others can. We'll suggest some questions for you to ask and point out some sources you can use.

The bottom line is this: As you choose a distance learning program, an obvious question is "Can I really take the courses from here, where I am?" More often than not, an important part of that question is "Can I really get the library services that I'll need here, where I am?" Good libraries and related information services are more available, have more material to offer, and are better prepared to work with you than ever before. Don't settle for less.

UPDATING TRADITION: TODAY'S LIBRARIES

The library has always been the student's friend. Whether you have a good library nearby or need to conduct all of your library work online, it's helpful to know some of the basics about these institutions and the people who work there.

What libraries are available? Your first choice is the library of the institution that's offering the distance education program. In addition, there may be a local public library. You might have access to libraries of nearby colleges and universities, or perhaps you have access to specialized resources, such as legal and medical libraries associated with local institutions. A look through the library listings of Yellow Pages and government pages in your local telephone directory may yield important resources. A few calls to nearby libraries will equip you with such basic information as hours of operation, checkout policies, or photocopy costs. And the home page of most state libraries includes links to all the libraries in the state that are Internet-accessible. A link to the state library page is usually available from your state government's Web page.

Academic Libraries

If you are investigating a college or university library, you will want to find out about the strengths of its book and journal collections. Does it collect materials in the field you want to study? One way to find out is to look at the college catalog and see if that subject area is taught there. Check the library for handouts that might give details about special collections it might have. Many large college libraries have extensive special collections, sometimes housed in a certain area of the library or even in a different building. The resources of these special collections are not always listed in the online catalog. In fact, a good question to ask any library is whether it has special resources appropriate to your work but not listed in the online catalog. You may find out about newly acquired items or treasures for which the library has lacked the resources to make fully public. You will also find that many large universities have a main library plus other specialized libraries around campus, which may have access and loan policies different from the main library.

Using Library Databases

Any tour of local libraries is sure to turn up interesting surprises. Many libraries have special databases, often on CD-ROM, which may be available only on select computers in the library. Do not assume that every computer in the library is the same or that all have the

same databases. Never assume that access to library databases from home equals that available in the library. Most libraries now have a variety of electronic databases. These databases are usually governed by license agreements, which may not allow more access or may provide it via special accounts. License restrictions or technical limitations may not allow certain databases to be networked and made available on multiple computers. Also, computers in the library may have special modifications to hardware or software that facilitate access and printing.

To receive service from some college libraries you must be enrolled in a course or have a computer account at the college. If you have a computer account, you may be allowed to dial in to the campus servers. This may get you access to special databases. Be creative—by taking an extension course or one regular course, you may get access to resources you can't buy! Also, some libraries have special corporate accounts. You might check at your place of employment to see if it has any such relationships established, and whether they might help provide access for your research.

Downloading Information

Ask about downloading or emailing the information you locate on library computers. Find out what programs you will need in order to read the files on your own computer at home. Can you dial in from home and download material from the library? Even if you can't, it may be possible for you to go to the library, access the material, then email it to yourself. If the library workstation you are using has an Internet browser loaded on it, mail and print features are probably available. Much more information about database access can be found later in this chapter.

Getting Help

If you intend to use library services extensively, get to know the people working in the reference, circulation, and interlibrary loan departments. Who should you talk to at a library to get the most informed service? During many hours of the day, students or part-time employees may staff the circulation or checkout desk. They generally receive some training, but if they can't answer your questions with assurance, try the reference desk. Reference librarians will know how to acquire special services and about special agreements with other libraries and colleges that may be helpful to you. If the library has a home page, there usually is a department or staff directory with phone numbers and often email addresses.

Librarians like to help. As with most jobs, the more uncommon the problem, the more interesting it becomes! Think about what you need help to find—statistics? books? journal articles? maps? video or audio materials? Every library is different. Most buy certain core reference materials, such as general encyclopedias, but from there, the variations begin. Some have special collections in specific areas. Some libraries will be depositories for local, state, or federal documents. If you have access to several libraries, you may have to do some research before you can determine which one has the resources most important to you.

TIP To get more help with complex questions, find times when the library is least busy—typically during the early morning or dinner hours. At college libraries, remember that many students do their research in the middle of the term (or at the last possible moment), inundating the library with special requests. If you can, schedule your research visits during quieter periods, perhaps calling for an appointment with a reference librarian. Service might be especially good between terms, since many college libraries remain open even when classes are not in session. Be sure to ask about operating hours between terms.

Smaller public and academic libraries are not equipped to provide the resources of a research university library, but if you plan your work carefully, they can help you locate materials and borrow what is needed from other libraries. Your local library, no matter how large or small, wants to help. Take time to know the resources and the staff. The payoff comes in shorter time lines and lower costs as you do your research.

The Online Catalog

Most library catalogs are now computerized; the traditional drawers of file cards are gone. The electronic catalog is more accurate, and listings are more likely to be current. It's easier, faster, and more powerful to use, since you can tailor your search quite precisely. Particularly important to distance students, the catalog may be available online to users beyond the library walls.

If you have access to the Internet, you have access to many more library catalogs than you realize. For example, if you check the Web site of the University of Saskatchewan libraries, you'll find a very

comprehensive service called WebCats: Library Catalogs on the World Wide Web. WebCats is easily reachable from this Guide's Web site. Internet-based resources will be discussed more thoroughly later in this chapter.

Access to Online Catalogs. If you're a long way from a library that you would like to use, the first question to ask is "Can I access the catalog from here?" If the answer is yes, the next obvious question is "How?" There are three possibilities:

1. You dial, using your modem, directly to the library's phone number for the online catalog.
2. You use your Web browser to access the library's Web site, which will direct you to the catalog.
3. You use the Internet to access the library's catalog via the Telnet function. Telnet, essentially, provides a link that enables you to operate a distant computer via your own keyboard. Not all Internet service providers (ISPs) include the Telnet function.

If you're dialing in directly, you will need to know the library system's terminal emulation type so that you can set your communication software, allowing your computer to talk to their computer. You will also need the library's log-in command with password. The library can give you simple directions, but don't expect much help in troubleshooting. Also, most small libraries have a very limited number of dial-in lines. Ask if there is a special disconnect sequence to hang up, so you leave the line free for the next patron.

If the library is on the Web, it may or may not have a Web interface to the catalog. If it doesn't, a Telnet feature will be needed to search the catalog. With Telnet, the menus are command-driven, not point and click. With command-driven menus, you must give the proper key commands. Usually these are indicated on a help page or at the bottom of the screen. There will be no graphics with this type of connection as it handles text only. Many useful locations—including some important government sites—still need Telnet. Your browser will probably have a Telnet program embedded in it that will automatically launch when you connect to a Telnet site. If you can't easily find a Telnet program, ask your local ISP.

Searching the Catalog. Once you are connected to an online library catalog, look to see what indexes can be searched. Indexes present no mysteries: You use sets of indexes every time you pick up the phone book. The white pages are an alphabetical index of names. The Yellow Pages are an index of "subjects," or services and products.

An online catalog is also a set of indexes. In the catalogs, you will find such index categories as "Author Search," "Title Search," or "Subject Search." If there are examples of each type of search, look at them for helpful clues on how to search. The subject search may be an index of "controlled headings." These are the authoritative subjects set by the Library of Congress or the National Library of Medicine, for example. Searching in this type of index may help you establish the correct terminology needed to search precisely and give you related subject headings.

The Catalog's Records.   In an online catalog, each entry has an electronic record that describes it. The record has information about the author, title, publisher, date, and subjects covered. In addition, some records include special notes about the material. A keyword index in an online catalog may search for a word or combination of words anywhere in the record. This is different from keyword searching in a database of full-text journal articles, where a keyword search will search the entire text of all the articles.

Narrowing the Search.   You may have the option to "limit" your search, that is, to add more "directions" to your search, in order to narrow it and remove unwanted titles. For example, you might choose to limit your search to items in English, or to items published after 1990. Other indexes in the catalog might allow you to search only periodical titles or video titles.

A Universe of Catalogs.   When you access the online resources of a major university library or a library consortium, a huge number of sources become available to you. Through the library Web site of the University of California at Berkeley, for example, you can locate thousands of library catalogs on the Internet. Through a keyword index, you can search by location and type of library.

A library consortium will have a union catalog, which includes the holdings of all the consortium's member libraries. For instance, OhioLink, one of the largest consortia, combines the holdings of over fifty academic libraries in Ohio and contains over six million records. The University of California system, called MELVYL, contains almost nine million unique titles. You'll find the Web addresses (URLs) of these and other major resources via the Guide's Web site.

Why might you need to search such a huge database? You may be researching a very specialized topic or a new topic about which little has been published. Materials that can help you are more likely to show up in such a huge database. Once you have identified the book, journal, or other materials you are looking for, you will need to submit an interlibrary loan request through your local library.

TIP

As you search, spelling is important! If you misspell a word in your search command, the search will turn up empty or with incorrect information.

Interlibrary Loans

A particularly important service—especially if you're a long way from a major library—is the interlibrary loan. When you're shopping for distance education programs, a key question is: "Will your library provide full interlibrary loan service to me, just as it would for on-campus students?"

In spite of all our electronic marvels, most books and journals are still available only in traditional print formats, and an interlibrary loan is the mechanism that enables libraries to find and loan that material, even when they don't own it themselves. Typically the library that owns the material will ship a book but send photocopies of journal articles.

There are some important fundamentals about this service, the first of which is that when your library borrows material for you, your library is responsible for it and would have to cover its cost if you lost it. Your library, therefore, has a strong interest in your handling the material properly and returning it on time. They haven't been known to break anybody's knees, but grades or transcripts have been held hostage.

Some smaller libraries are reluctant to provide this service because it consumes scarce time and resources. Once you're assured that interlibrary loans are routine and welcome, your next questions are:

- How do I order an item? Can requests be sent via email?
- What is the cost? (Interlibrary loans may not be part of a library's free service.)
- How long does it take, and how am I notified that the material is in?

The usual interlibrary loan is from one library to another library and then to you. Some libraries are now arranging to send material directly to the person requesting it (thus saving you considerable time), but generally they do not ship direct to the patron. When using interlibrary loans, be realistic about your research deadlines: The process of locating, ordering, and delivering your material can take from a few days to six weeks.

Check on penalties for lost or late books. If something happens to the materials you borrow from a library, replacement fees could be very costly. You could also lose library privileges. Be sure to ask about how to return material and whether you can renew items. Generally, most items received through interlibrary loan have limited or no renewal available.

What if you are in an area with no interlibrary loan service? You may have to travel to the nearest large town with a good public library or college library. For either type of library, you will need a library card. Ask the college library what services you get with a card and how long the card is valid. Many libraries offer cards to those outside their service areas for a fee. Costs can vary from as little as $10 to over $100. Private colleges and universities may have more restrictive access policies than public colleges and universities. Most will do what they can to help you even if you are not taking classes from them.

GETTING THE MATERIAL—NOW

You may be taking a course from a very distant college, but you probably need the same library service as the people who are on campus. You don't want to take forever to locate the material you need, and then wait for it to be delivered. When you're considering a college, university, or other institution offering courses at a distance, you need to know that their library—or a very good substitute—will be there for you, wherever you are and whenever you need it.

Some libraries with excellent collections, both paper and electronic, must restrict their use to people who are physically in the library. Others offer online services, but not to all their online databases. The reasons are largely economic: The licenses that control the library's use of this material require that access be limited to a defined set of users, and sometimes that doesn't include you. Also, some libraries don't have the equipment or phone lines to serve people at a distance.

However, an increasing number of libraries provide good service at a distance. Some libraries will fax documents or provide special shipping arrangements on request. They may need to charge for some of these services, so you'll want to check your options. This is another question for the provider of your distance education program: What can your library do for me?

There are many databases you can access and search without any charges; you pay a fee only to order materials. You can then request delivery of items in any number of ways: regular mail, fax, package delivery, or courier services. For example, one such database is UnCover, which provides indexing of over 17,000 journals and their articles. For a fee, you can order articles directly from UnCover.

Some libraries are using new types of document delivery systems that speed the transfer of materials. One system, called Ariel, transfers scanned documents over the Internet. New versions of this program will allow delivery directly to the student through email. Your hardware and software may limit the quality of the transfer, so be sure to check with the interlibrary loan office about this option.

The Internet and the World Wide Web offer other options. You can order books online, for example from Amazon.com or Barnes & Noble. Some books no longer under copyright restrictions are available online. Our companion Web site has links to many sources. Try,

for example, Where the Wild Things Are: Librarian's Guide to the Best Information on the Net, which in turn will steer you to a great many useful resources.

Questions to Ask a Distance Education Provider About Library Services

How do you judge whether a college or a given library can offer you the service you'll need? The possibilities range from an electronic "reserve book room," ready to deliver online the material prescribed for your course by your instructor, to more limited service that is restricted to people who can do their work within the library walls. One measure of quality service: When you call the library at the institution offering your program, an easily reachable person, knowledgeable about distance education, should be there to help.

Evaluating Databases.   Most libraries subscribe to various electronic databases. Evaluating them can be complicated since there are major differences in what these databases index, how well they handle

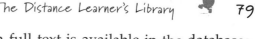

complex searches, how much full text is available in the databases, and how easy they are to use.

Questions to Ask a Librarian Concerning Helpful Databases

1 How many publications does this database index?

2 What percentage are available full text or full image? (For an explanation of full text and full image, see the section, "Specialized Databases," elsewhere in this chapter.)

3 What publications in my field of study are represented in this database?

4 How many of these titles are available in full text or full image?

5 How far back are these titles indexed?

Consider one prominent example. The Online Computer Library Center, Inc. (universally known by its initials, OCLC) has a product called FirstSearch. It provides access to more than 100 databases in many disciplines. Some of the databases have full text online. FirstSearch allows you to order the article and have it sent by fax or regular U. S. mail if you have an account. Many public and academic libraries offer FirstSearch to their users. Ask the reference or information desk.

Other major database vendors include UMI, which produces ProQuest; EbscoHost; Ovid; and Information Access Company, which produces Expanded Academic Index. Find out which are available for you to use.

If you have no access to databases like these, you are at a severe disadvantage in comparison with on-campus students.

Evaluating Library Service.   To what extent can you expect high-quality library service from the institution providing your distance education program? How much can you rely on local libraries to supply you with needed resources? These are areas of supreme importance if you are interested in quality education. You should have the answers to some serious questions and be comfortable with your options before you pay for the courses.

1 Is there a librarian who works with distance education students?

2 How do I get a computer account in order to access the institution's email and database services?

3 What interlibrary loan services are available?

  ▪ How quickly are items delivered?
  ▪ Where are these delivered? Can they be shipped directly to me?

4 What reference desk services are available?

  ▪ Who answers questions, and can I use email, telephone, or fax?
  ▪ Is the telephone number toll-free?
  ▪ How quickly are email or faxed questions answered?

5 Is there an orientation to the library services offered from the provider?

6 Are there special online resources available to me if I enroll in your program?

7 Are there arrangements with local libraries so that I can use them as "extensions" of the provider's library?

You should consider a different distance education provider if you cannot get good answers to these questions in a timely manner.

USING THE INTERNET AND THE WORLD WIDE WEB

You have identified the resources available to you through the institution providing your distance education program, or through your local public or college libraries, but there are other possibilities. What is available to you on the Internet? Once you have access to the hardware and software discussed in Chapter 3 of this book, sitting in front of a computer connected to the Internet, browser at the ready, where do you go? How do you know that what you find is authoritative and not propaganda? How can you know whether you've found the best information available? How do you get access to important databases that cost money?

First, you should know some myths about online information. Some people seem to believe that all information is available somewhere on the World Wide Web. Not so. Another myth is that everything on the Internet is free. Hardly. Sometimes portions of commercial copyrighted material may appear, but often it is there to entice you to go out and purchase the complete information. Many information sites have home pages, but to access and search the data, you will need an account or subscription.

And certainly all that is out there is not reliable. One leading medical journal, the *Journal of the American Medical Association*, commented:

> The problem is not too little information but too much, vast chunks of it incomplete, misleading, or inaccurate, and not only in the medical area. The Net—and especially the Web—has the potential to become the world's largest vanity press. It is a medium in which anyone with a computer can serve simultaneously as author, editor, and publisher and can fill any or all of those roles anonymously if he or she so chooses. In such an environment, novices and savvy Internet users alike can have trouble distinguishing the wheat from the chaff, the useful from the harmful.[1]

Yes indeed! There are Web sites based on everything from rumor and innuendo to outright fantasy, which all appear to be "information." Some cues to quality control will be described later.

Searching the Internet.   You can use the Internet to search virtually any topic or issue. You may have a known Web site to visit, but most of the time you will want to find out what's available about the subject at hand. There are two different ways to approach the search for information on the World Wide Web: looking through directories and using search engines. Some sites blend the two and even offer something called "meta-searching," which is a method for searching multiple search engines. Web resources are, to say the least, dynamic: New stars appear and old friends fade away. You will find an up-to-date guide with hyperlinks to many of the best current resources—including those mentioned in this chapter—at the Web site that accompanies this Guide. Meanwhile, the following sections provide some good starting points.

Directories and Libraries.   A good first stop is the structured directory in Yahoo! By following the directories to narrower and narrower areas or topics, you can arrive at a list of resources on the Internet, all

---

[1] "Assessing, controlling, and assuring the quality of medical information on the Internet: *caveat lector et viewor*—let the reader and viewer beware." Editorial, William A. Silberg, George D. Lundberg, and Robert Musacchio, *The Journal of the American Medical Association*, 1997; 277 (15): 1244.

directly related to a topic or subject area. The Argus Clearinghouse is another example of a good directory.

Some directories of Web pages offer sites carefully selected according to some criteria for inclusion. Many library home pages offer links to special resources grouped by subject. Try, for example, The Internet Public Library. It's a good attempt by librarians to bring some order to the Internet.

You can connect to several other important sources via our Web site. Some examples:

- The Scholars' Guide to WWW is good for humanities research.
- My Virtual Reference Desk offers many useful links that are regularly checked.
- You'll find particularly good science links in Martindale's The Reference Desk.
- As we mentioned earlier, Where the Wild Things Are: Librarian's Guide to the Best Information on the Net is a fine collection of sites from St. Ambrose University's librarians. It has an electronic reading room and links to full-text sites and online bookstores.
- And recall the earlier references to libraries' and library consortia's online catalogs, including "WebCats" at the University of Saskatchewan libraries, the University of California at Berkeley, "Ohiolink," and "MELVYL."

Search Engines.   Along with Internet directories and library reference sources, you can locate information by using one of the search engines available on the Internet. These engines have different features, and they search different parts of the Internet. It's a good idea to look at some of the comparisons of search engines available in print and on the Internet. First, you should know the basic principles common to most of the engines. Then you will know how to structure your search to retrieve the best available information for your work.

Some Search Engine Basics.   Most search engines have some common features. It is helpful to know these basics so you can create good searches. Use quotation marks to enclose a phrase where the words must appear together, for example, **"ocean kayak."** A truncation symbol is helpful in expanding the search term: **"ocean kayak*"** The star symbol tells the computer to accept the words "kayak," "kayaks," or "kayaking." You can narrow the search with the "+" or "−" symbol: **"ocean kayak*"+Hawaii** retrieves documents with "ocean kayak*" and "Hawaii" in them. Searching **"ocean kayak*"–festival** leaves out documents with the word "festival" in them.

Constructing a solid search depends upon two things: the features of the search engine, and your ability to work with the terms you want to search. The best way to learn is to try some searches, read the help pages offered on the home pages of the search engines, and look at some of the sites mentioned below. That will help you understand the power and limitations of the search engines. We have mentioned only a few basic search techniques here.

WARNING! Searching is fun, but effective searching is not easy. You will need to learn how to construct a search and how the different search engines work. Plan to try three or four different engines. You will want to practice some searches on them until you're confident that you can quickly compose an effective search. Here are some search engines and a few hints about using them:

- When you try HotBot, go to the help pages to learn the basics and the "Super search" method.

- AltaVista is a longtime favorite search engine with good help pages and a nice "refine" option that allows you to alter your search easily. Also, try WebCrawler.

- Northern Light has a "Special Collection" feature in which you can run searches in over 2,900 journals, magazines, and newswire services and have the articles sent to you.

- The "Internet Search Tools" page from the Library of Congress has links to all types of searching tools for the Internet, including the metasearch tools that simultaneously search several search engines. Included are some sites that compare those tools.

- Ten Steps to Internet Searching is Ernest Ackermann's useful site. His list of 10 steps to Internet searching is a good reason to visit this site. And don't miss the other valuable nuggets, such as his tips on evaluating Web sites.

Specialized Databases. There are special databases on the Internet where you can perform detailed searches for specific information. You can find many of these databases listed at the site of the University of California at Berkeley. Particularly valuable for medical research is Medline; most American medical journals are indexed here, and many important foreign journals are included. Searching is free.

UnCover, mentioned earlier, is the all-purpose database for journal article citations on any number of topics. It indexes over 17,000 journals back to 1988. Before you pay for quick-service full-text delivery of articles, check to see if that journal is available at one of your local libraries or through interlibrary loan.

Internet Sleuth has links to over 2,000 databases divided by categories such as Arts & Humanities and Sciences.

In searching databases, be aware that the content may be citations and abstracts, or it may include the content of articles. The content may not be complete. Full text usually means you get the text of articles, but no pictures, graphs, charts, or illustrations of any kind. Full image generally has the article nearly as it appears in print. Such documents may be downloaded, but they may require a special reader program; for example, the files may use Adobe Acrobat. The reader program is available free for almost every type of computer at many places on the Internet.

Sometimes subscribing to a newspaper, magazine, or journal gets you privileged electronic access. You might find it cost-effective to subscribe to a journal or newspaper that gives you a password into its databases. Often you can search back issues or obtain access to special information only available to subscribers. You might check with your librarian to learn if the library subscribes to the journal or paper—it may have received a password. A librarian then can search for you—probably the library can't give out the password. Important resources such as the *Wall Street Journal* and *The New York Times* have this feature.

Internet Training.　There are classes that teach Internet searching. Your local library or college may offer some. Sometimes you can find library courses and tutorials online. For example, there's a site managed by the library faculty at the University of California at Berkeley, which is designed to teach effective Internet search strategies. The site is regularly updated with the latest teaching tips direct from classroom testing. There are links to all the search engines, but more importantly, there are instructions for how to—and how not to—search. Specific directions are included to guide you in constructing searches in the major engines and metasearch engines. Instructions for effectively investigating directories such as Yahoo! can be found here also. Beyond General Internet Searching has links to Virtual Reference Libraries and Full-Text Resource Locators.

Useful library skill courses are available on the Web complete with lessons and assignments. You can link there directly from our site. The lessons cover Internet searching, common databases, and many helpful tips on using libraries.

Determining the Quality of What You Find.   You've located some information, but how reliable is it? Is it authoritative, unbiased, and backed up with solid evidence? What are some useful criteria for evaluating sites? You can begin with some of the qualifiers you would use for a print source:

- Who is the author?
- What are the author's credentials?
- Is he affiliated with an institution?
- Does the author document her sources?
- What evidence is brought to support the information?
- If statistics are cited, are the sources provided?
- How current is the material and when was the site last updated?
- What's the nature of the site? You can determine whether it's associated with government, education, an organization, or a commercial company by looking for **.gov, .edu, .org,** or **.com** in the site address.

You can use the Internet to find out more about the author and the institutions with which he or she may be affiliated by searching for an author's home pages or using a search engine to locate their publications. Especially in the sciences, recent publications may appear on the Internet. Searching a journal citation index like UnCover might reveal other publications by the author.

The information on your distance learning provider's Web site should be considered accurate. Most information on educational institutions' academic "official" pages is accurate. BEWARE: Most educational institutions provide space for "personal" pages for faculty, staff, and students. So the Web page you're looking at from that prestigious university may have been put up by a student who, with good intentions, has "published" inaccurate information. Even faculty "personal" pages may be an expression of an individual's thoughts or beliefs and may not be generally accepted in his profession. Commercial and organizational sites can be similarly misleading.

There are several good guides for evaluating Internet resources. *Searching and Researching on the Internet and the World Wide Web* is a site that accompanies the book of the same name by Ernest Ackermann and Karen Hartman, published by Franklin, Beedle & Associates, 1997. The site includes a good glossary and links to helpful information on using the Internet and the Web. You can link to it directly from our Web site.

SUMMARY: QUESTIONS AND CHOICES

As you choose a distance learning program, an obvious question is "Can I really take the courses from here?" More often than not, an important part of that question is "How can I get the library services that I'll need?"

Some courses are essentially self-contained with all necessary material provided and no need for library support. Most, however, require some independent digging for information, and for that, you'll need a library that can supply what you need, when you need it, with no more out-of-pocket cost than necessary.

In this chapter, we've reviewed your prospective options and some of the pertinent questions for you to ask providers and libraries. In summary, it may be helpful to list some of the most important issues:

1 I'm considering a distance education program from College X.

- Can I access the college library's catalog online?
- Can I have online access to the same electronic resources that are available to students who visit the library?
- Are reference librarians available to me? May I send questions and requests by phone, email, or fax? What's the likely response time to an email or fax request?
- Will the college library ship material to me?
- Is there an electronic reserve reading room for my prospective course? Can I access it from here with the hardware and software that are available to me?
- Will the college library get material for me by interlibrary loan? If so, how will I receive the material? How long will it take? Will there be some cost involved?
- Will the course material be available in a nearby learning center affiliated with the college?
- Is there a distance education librarian available to help?

2 If College X's library can't provide these services, is there another option available? A nearby public library? Another academic library? What services can they provide? Are these services appropriate for my program? What would they cost?

3 To what extent might Internet searches fulfill my library requirements? How would I get access to the databases I need, and at what cost?

Such a list of questions may seem daunting, but you don't want to be blindsided—you don't want to register for a program and then find that you can't get the books, documents, or online information that you need. The old saw "Better safe than sorry" is germane. In fact, the institutions that offer the best distance education programs have good answers to these questions, and you'll find that a rapidly increasing number of libraries are prepared to provide the service you need.

As we said at the beginning of this chapter, today's library is a major key to the information age, and today's librarians may be the distance learner's best friends.

UNDERSTANDING YOUR NEEDS

Overcoming the Personal Barriers to Success in Distance Learning

In this chapter you will

- learn to clarify your goals for being a student and participating in distance learning

- learn to understand your attitudes toward distance learning

- discover how to prioritize your roles and responsibilities so that being a student is high on the list

- find ways to identify and develop support systems within your distance learning courses—both virtual and face to face

- learn to value health as important to goal achievement and course success

Students who succeed in distance learning are able to focus on their goals, prioritize their responsibilities, reach out for the assistance they need, and pay attention to their health. This chapter is designed to help you develop the skills of other successful distance learners.

LEARNING FROM OTHERS

You know the old saying "Hindsight is 20/20." Scattered throughout this chapter are stories and "sidebars of advice" obtained from the experiences of distance learners. Their purpose is to let you learn from the hindsight of others who have attempted and succeeded in distance learning. These anecdotes should provide you with information about how to succeed and some perspective on how to handle the personal challenges of being a college student at a distance.

WHERE TO LEARN MORE

There are a number of resources to pursue if you wish to explore in more detail any of the topics covered in this chapter. The resources include both print and nonprint information and, for the most part, are just the tip of the iceberg. These resources will be updated regularly on the Guide's Web site. The references consulted in preparing this chapter are also listed on the Guide's Web site.

TIP Advice from Other Distance Learners

When asked what advice they would give to others who were about to participate in distance learning, students in a variety of undergraduate and graduate television classes had the following responses:

- Be committed—give it all you have!
- Participate—ask questions—pay attention.
- Be familiar with a computer.
- Form a "buddy system" or small groups to support each other.
- Be prepared to work independently.

CLARIFYING YOUR GOALS AND ATTITUDES

Why Do You Want to Be a Student and, in Particular, a Distance Learner?

Students who don't have at least some idea why they are in college are more likely to drop out or find themselves in academic difficulty. So it makes sense for you to have an idea (even if it is preliminary) as to why you want to take college courses and, in particular, distance learning courses. Asking yourself three basic questions will help you clarify your goals and attitudes:

- Why do you want to be a student?
- Why do you want to participate in distance learning?
- What are your attitudes toward distance learning?

Why Do You Want to Be a Student?   There are a variety of reasons people give for being a student. The following list contains a few of these reasons, but there are many more.

- to help in a current job
- to move toward a new job or career change
- to move toward a college degree and a career
- to retain an ability to do a particular job (e.g., licensing issues)
- because friends are students
- because it's the thing to do after high school
- to learn about a particular topic (personal enrichment)

These reasons reflect the *value* that people place on the importance of being a student. For example, if you need courses to be able to keep your job, being a student will have a different value (and priority) than if you don't need college courses and have no particular need or desire for a degree. *What are your reasons for being a student?* For this question and the others in this section, indicate your reasons in the blanks provided or use Worksheet #1 on our Web site.

_____

_____

_____

_____

_____

_____

Why Do You Want to Participate in Distance Learning?   There are many different reasons for choosing distance learning. Some of the more common ones are

- saving on travel time
- convenient to my schedule
- desire to try a new learning situation
- preference to learn independently
- interest in the topic or content being offered
- content not offered in a traditional, campus-based setting
- cannot attend campus classes

How about you? *Why are you interested in distance learning?*

_____

_____

_____

_____

_____

_____

What Are Your Attitudes Toward Distance Learning?   Attitudes toward course content affect your interest in and approach to learning (for example, the "math-phobic" person). Attitudes toward course delivery systems can also affect your interest in, approach to, and success in learning. How does your reason for participating in distance learning influence your motivation to learn? Does it? For example, if your preference is to take courses in a traditional, campus-based classroom setting but the course you want or need is not offered in that form, how will this affect your interest and motivation to learn? *What are your attitudes toward distance learning?*

_____

_____

_____

_____

_____

_____

Putting It Together. Worksheet #1, "Clarifying Your Goals and Attitudes" (see the Web site), has been designed for you to record your answers to the three basic questions discussed above. Your answers to the first two questions will be useful in setting your priorities. The responses you give regarding your attitudes toward distance learning may require further action on your part. For example, if you are quite skeptical about distance learning, review the first chapter of this Guide; sometimes we are skeptical because we don't have enough information. If after learning more about distance learning you remain skeptical, determine whether the concerns you have will interfere with your learning in the course. If they will, perhaps distance learning is not the mode for you. Remember, you know yourself better than anyone! *Being honest in your assessment is the best way to ensure your success!*

THE ESSENCE OF BEING HUMAN: TOO MANY ROLES, TOO LITTLE TIME

Advice from One Distance Learner

TIP Be aware that if you are not willing to use time management and set priorities, then distance learning is not going to work for you. You are making a commitment. Be aware that you will need to make lifestyle choices.

Successful distance learners are able to prioritize their commitments effectively. This involves understanding and juggling the multiple roles we play as human beings. For many of us, these are almost impossible tasks.

Being human in modern society means that we find ourselves wearing many different "hats." In sociology, these hats are referred to as *roles*. Roles are often thought of in terms of titles or positions (e.g., mother, engineer, vice president, Little League coach). We use such terms daily to describe others and ourselves. As each of us assumes a new role, we usually undertake the responsibilities and expected actions that *we think are necessary* to succeed in this new role.

Think about yourself in the role of worker. What do you expect of yourself? What behaviors or actions do you need to perform in order to be considered—by yourself and perhaps others—as an effective worker? You can look at any role and ask yourself the same questions. What you will find quickly, and perhaps be surprised by, is that you play many different roles in your life; each role carries a set of expectations regarding behavior, and some roles have a higher priority than others.

For example, you may be an employee for some organization, while simultaneously being a parent, a spouse, a friend, a brother or sister, or a volunteer. Since you are reading this Guide, you are also currently or potentially a *student*. Given all your roles, you already realize that it is becoming difficult to accomplish everything you need and want to do within the time you have to do it. How can you possibly take on anything else, especially something that is as time-consuming as being a student?

From Chaos to Order: Determining Opportunity Costs

To bring order to the chaos of our lives, and to make room for new roles such as student, we need to acknowledge the various roles we play and make decisions about each role's importance to us. In essence, we need to *prioritize*. Prioritizing is a critical process as you take on the role of student, and it is even more important when you are a student learning at a distance. Unfortunately, prioritizing roles tends to be an informal process, performed without considering all its consequences. As harsh as it sounds (and sometimes is), taking on the role of student may mean that you have to give up, or at least temporarily postpone, something else. REMEMBER: You're prioritizing in anticipation of some reward in the end—course completion, college degree, job promotion, and others.

Making decisions about priorities requires you to determine the value of adding the role of student to your life and weighing it against the value of what you will have to give up or postpone in order to take on the role. To ensure your success, the role of student needs to have value to you and to occupy a high priority in your life. The basic question for you to ask yourself is: *"Is taking on the role of student worth it to me—and why?"*

Avoiding Murphy's Law: Prioritizing and Negotiating Role Commitments and Responsibilities

Most likely the role commitments that will interfere with your studies fall into the "work" and "family" categories because these roles are often viewed as the most important and most difficult to postpone. According to Murphy's Law, you can anticipate that something will go awry during your distance learning course. However, this shouldn't stop you from pursuing distance learning. By prioritizing and negotiating with significant others, you can increase your capacity to accommodate the inevitable crisis and help ensure your success as a learner.

In setting your priorities to incorporate the role of student, refer back to your answers about why you want to be a student and why you want to participate in distance learning. Then, applying the priority-setting process outlined in the next few pages, answer the following question: *"How important is being a student compared to the other important things in my life?"*

This evaluation is essential to being able to successfully manage your time and maneuver around any crisis that may occur. Goal setting and priority setting are critical parts of your plan for educational success. All too often we neglect these processes because we think we can handle anything that comes our way. Foresight and forethought are *always* better than hindsight in the case of college success.

Priority Setting as Life Management

Sometimes the process of setting priorities is considered a form of time management. While prioritizing your roles and responsibilities can be considered the first step in developing a day-to-day or weekly time management plan, it is also a form of *life management*.

Before you map out a detailed daily or weekly time management plan, you should decide whether you are ready, and able, to take the class or classes in the first place. This involves defining your role commitments, prioritizing them according to their value or importance to you, and estimating the amount of time you need to devote to them each week. There are many different systems you can use; some are included in the resources for this chapter. Next, we'll explain a quick and simple approach to making decisions about your role priorities.

Three Steps to Setting Your Priorities

In prioritizing your roles, you need to

1. list the major roles you play
2. rate the importance of each role to you using a simple rating scale
3. determine how much time you spend each week engaged in each role activity

The amount of time you spend on a priority role should coincide with the importance of that priority to you. Worksheets #2 and #3 have been developed to help you understand your roles and priorities—both as student and nonstudent. These worksheets are available on the Guide's Web site for you to download and use.

To show you how easy, yet important, understanding your roles and priorities is to your academic success, an example of how one student engaged in this process is provided. By working through Worksheets #2 and #3, Cheryl was able to identify what was truly important to her and what she felt she could and could not "give up" in order to take her course successfully.

A Process in Action: Cheryl's Experience

Cheryl is a married professional woman with a 10-month-old child. Her husband is also a professional, and both devote 50–60 hours per week in their jobs, which happen to be with the same company. Day care is provided on site, and their child is enrolled, so there are opportunities for each of them to visit during the day if desired or necessary. Cheryl decided that she really needed to explore a different career field that would allow her to spend more time

(continued)

with their child. As a family, they have become accustomed to a particular lifestyle, so a major salary reduction was not possible, although some reduction would be okay. As a result of the joint decision for Cheryl to begin to explore other career options, Cheryl decided to "test the waters" by taking a college course that would move her in a new direction. The course she wanted was a late evening course. The course description indicated that there was much independent work as well as a required group project. No one in the class lived closer than 30 minutes from the site, with many living as far away as an hour. Participating in the course would mean that Cheryl would be away from home at least one evening a week (her job also required her to be away from home at times) and that she would have to devote time to doing the course assignments. Given a more than full-time job and her family responsibilities, Cheryl needed to set some priorities. Here's how she completed Worksheet #2:

Cheryl's Worksheet #2
Understanding Your Roles and Priorities
(without the role of student)

Role	Perceived Priority (Rate in order of importance with 1 being the most important)					Time Spent on Activity Each Week
	1	2	3	4	5	
Work (manager, employee)	X					60
Family (parent & wife)	X					42
Friends/Social		X				6
Leisure (reading, watching TV)			X			10
Other						
Volunteer			X			2
	Subtotal time					120
	Add hours you sleep					+48*
	Total time					168

*Includes naps with child.

(continued)

With all of her time accounted for in these roles, it was clear to Cheryl that something needed to shift so she could be successful in taking her class. Through discussions with her husband, they renegotiated the time each spent with their child. At work, through task delegation, Cheryl was able to reduce her schedule by five hours per week. She also decided that her role as a volunteer would need to be put on hold for at least this semester. Reducing her sleep time and leisure time were not options for Cheryl. The time she slept included the minimum amount of sleep she needed to feel rested (six hours per night) and the amount of time she devoted to getting her child to sleep. Her leisure time was a way for her to unwind and, since it was already minimal, not viewed as something that could be reduced. As a couple, they also agreed to temporarily cut back on their weekend get-togethers with their friends from two to three times a month to no more than twice. These reordered priorities provided Cheryl with the time she needed to do her course work and enabled her to accommodate the crisis she experienced when a family member became seriously ill. She contributed to her group assignments, through email as well as fax, and she ended up with an "A" in the course. Her reordered priorities are reflected in Worksheet #3:

Cheryl's Worksheet #3
Building the Role of Student into Your Roles and Priorities

Role	Perceived Priority (Rate in order of importance with 1 being the most important)					Time Spent on Activity Each Week
	1	2	3	4	5	
Work (manager, employee)	X					55
Family (parent & wife)	X					32
Friends/Social			X			4
Leisure (reading, watching TV)		X				10
Other						
Student	X					19*
	Subtotal time					120
*Includes travel time.	Add hours you sleep					+48†
†Includes naps with child.	Total time					168

By devoting some time to setting and negotiating her roles and priorities, Cheryl was able to identify what was truly important to her and what she felt she could and could not "give up" in order to take and be successful in her course. Try completing the worksheets yourself. A couple of general guidelines should help you:

- Remember there are **only** 168 hours in a week.
- A general rule-of-thumb for anticipating how much time a college course will take is to equate a three-credit undergraduate course to about 10 hours per week. This includes time in formal instruction (if there is any) and study time. Not all courses fit this guideline, but it is a good place to start.

Listed below are the types of questions asked throughout this section and a few more to help you make your decisions about distance learning.

- What are your reasons for being a student?
- Why do you want to participate in distance learning?
- What roles do you currently play and how do they rate in importance in relationship to one another?
- How important is being a student compared to your other roles and responsibilities?
- What role priorities can be adjusted to accommodate your student role? Taking distance learning courses requires more independent learning than on-campus courses. How do you plan to adjust for this? What roles are *absolute* and cannot be changed versus roles that *can be adjusted* with acceptable consequences? Additional questions to ask yourself as you evaluate and prioritize your roles include:
  - How much will you be working? Is this required or a preference for you?
  - How much sleep do you require to be at your best?
  - Are you a morning, afternoon, or evening person—when are you at your best for learning? This is good information to have to help you determine the time of day that is optimal for you to take courses.
  - What about your leisure time and social life? How can you make sure that you preserve at least some of these positive activities?

- Can you anticipate any situations that may pose problems for you during the course of your distance learning experience—family illness, job changes, relocation, and so forth? Are these situations that are easily accommodated or not? It is impossible to anticipate all issues that might come up, nor is it very healthy to focus on what might go wrong. However, if you know of situations that may affect your ability to complete your course(s) successfully, it is important to consider and plan for these events. Remember the comment about foresight and forethought.

A little preplanning can go a long way to bolster your motivation and commitment to pursuing distance learning. The exercises, advice, and examples offered here are designed to help you to understand quickly the importance of goal clarification and prioritizing roles as well as to provide you with an easy way to implement these processes for yourself.

DEVELOPING SYSTEMS OF SUPPORT

We gave a lot of attention to goal setting and priority setting as a way to help ensure your distance learning success because it is an important process! However, there are other important areas in your role as student. For example, being able to connect with faculty members, other students, and academic support, such as tutoring, is very important to many distance learners. Once you've committed to a distance learning course, how do you go about connecting with others when learning at a distance? Also, if you find you need academic assistance, how do you go about getting it?

In a traditional college course that meets routinely with students and faculty in the same room, classroom interaction (or the potential for interaction) is always present. It is also somewhat easy for those who routinely travel to a campus to take advantage of the learning resources that might be available. The potential for interaction and connection may not be as easy when the course is offered through distance learning. When contact with faculty members, other students, or campus resources is either limited or nonexistent, you need to be assertive and creative in finding ways to interact and connect to support your learning. What follows are suggestions for initiating and developing systems of support to meet your needs as a distance learner.

Connecting and Communicating with Other Students and Faculty Members

TIP Make sure you know someone in the class with whom you can brainstorm, discuss problems, etc. Try to implement a buddy system.

If one of the reasons you chose distance learning is because of the independence of the learning situation, having contact with other students and faculty members may not be an issue. For many students, however, this interaction is important and is positively linked to their academic success. So, it is important to make it possible for distance learners to connect with faculty members and other students either routinely or on an as-needed basis.

Creating Your Own "Community of Learners"

There are a number of ways to create a team of learners to support you in your distance learning courses. A few of the obvious ones are listed here. Additional information, particularly about those possibilities that involve technology, were discussed in Chapter 3.

Sharing Students' and Faculty Members' Names, Addresses, Phone Numbers, and Email Addresses.   Ask the faculty member teaching the course to prepare and distribute the names, addresses, phone numbers, and email addresses of students taking the course. She will, of course, need to get permission directly from the students to do this.

Email Addresses.   Ask the faculty member or the institution about email addresses. Are you eligible to receive an email address through the institution? How do you get one? If you already have one, can you use it on this institution's system? The use of email will make it easier for you to connect with your faculty member and other students in your class.

Listservs.   Sometimes instructors have special computer-based Listservs created for courses. They use these as a way to communicate by email with their students and to respond to individual questions and concerns. Ask your instructor whether there will be a Listserv. If not, ask the instructor to consider it as a way for students to interact easily with him and other students.

Geographically Based Study Groups. Through a sharing of names and addresses, and by using a Listserv, groups of students can be identified that can emerge as learning communities. For example, if you find a few other students who are taking your course that live within a reasonable commuting distance from a central point, you may find that you can create a study support group.

Feedback Network. You may not want or be able to meet regularly with other students. Telephones and regular mail remain useful tools to establish connections and feedback from others in your distance learning courses.

Sharon's story, on the following page, addresses how she developed her priorities and juggled her multiple roles while being a distance learner. It also stresses how essential it was for her to connect with other students and faculty members.

For Sharon, who views herself as an independent learner, it was knowing that support and feedback was available (through faculty contact and/or student contact) that was important. At times, she took advantage of it; at others, she didn't.

Connecting with Learning Resources

TIP For success with content:

- Be very involved in the class.
- Stay on top of the work.
- Ask questions if you don't understand.

Even the best students may need help with course content from time to time! As a distance learner, you may have to be a little creative in finding ways to facilitate getting the help you need. This section offers some possibilities and questions for you to explore to help you get the help you might need.

First, review your own study habits using the information in Chapter 6. Are you approaching the study of the material in a way that will help you understand it and reinforce your long-term memory? Those who regularly work with students in the area of academic assistance often find that many students don't require content support. They just need to evaluate and adjust their study habits and/or weekly time management plan.

Second, if you find that you do need assistance with understanding the content and/or concepts of a course, find out what possibilities exist for you. Pursue the items on page 104 with your faculty member.

A Process in Action: The Development of Academic Support Through Feedback

Sharon is a married professional woman with two children in college. She is working on a graduate degree—taking two courses—in addition to working full time. Sharon and her husband have gone through many negotiations regarding roles and responsibilities over the years. Indeed, she believes that having a solid base of family support and sharing of responsibilities are essential to succeeding in college and, in particular, distance learning.

Sharon pursued her undergraduate degree while her children were young and found that it was really difficult trying to do everything that needed to be done and spend time with her family. The highest priority for Sharon was her family, and she found that the adjustments she made in her role priorities were in the areas related to her own leisure activities. The same has been true for her graduate work. Consequently, she sometimes feels as if she is "burning the candle at both ends" and is exhausted by the end of a term. She says that during any term she keeps repeating to herself, "It's only for a short time," to help get her through to the end.

Not unlike many distance learners, Sharon found taking a course through distance learning to be convenient to her schedule. For her, the trade-off in convenience more than made up for the lack of face-to-face interaction. Her most recent distance learning course was a television course she took at a receive site at the elementary school in her hometown. There was one other person at the receive site.

Sharon did well in the course and believes that support, particularly in the form of feedback, is very important in letting students know how well they are doing. She found that while the faculty member did distribute the names and addresses of all students taking the course at all locations, she relied mostly upon the conversations she had with the other person at the site for her source of support when she needed it. The two of them were able to discuss issues and provide some of the feedback that, at times, because of the large number of students taking the class, seemed slow in coming from the instructor.

- **Ask your faculty member for assistance.** She may be able to guide you to resources that will help you. Asking questions is important! If you are having difficulty, other students may be having trouble as well. If you don't voice your concerns and need for assistance, your faculty member will never know that there is a problem.

- **Is there a study guide for the course that will help you with understanding the content?** Perhaps the faculty member has developed one or could recommend one.

- **Does the host institution offer tutoring, on-site and/or virtual, for the content area?** Perhaps the faculty member has designed ways to provide learning assistance support to students.

- **Are there computer software programs available, which you could purchase, to help you with the content?**

To summarize, participating in distance learning does not mean you are totally on your own. There are ways to connect with faculty members and other students to develop small learning communities for mutual support. In the event you need academic assistance, there are avenues for you to pursue to get the help you need. Here are some questions you can ask yourself, faculty members, and institutions as you explore your own needs for connection and support and how to get those needs met.

- What are your preferences regarding contact with faculty members and other students? Are you more of an independent learner than not? If not, does the course you are taking or contemplating provide you with the opportunities, virtual and otherwise, for interaction with others that you need?

- What kinds of learning assistance are available to distance learning students? Are campus-based services open to those in distance learning? What provisions have been made to support those who might be having difficulty with content who do not live within commuting distance to the host institution?

Expecting Support and Assistance Is Okay

What is important to remember is that although you may not be on campus, you are a student taking a course or courses from an institution. It is perfectly acceptable to express your needs for communication with faculty members and other students as well as for learning assistance. It is also perfectly reasonable to expect that if resources are made available to other students served by the institution, they might also be available in some form to you as a distance learner. You should evaluate your needs and determine what the institution provides to meet them. Be aware that not all institutions will be able to provide the services you may want or need. They should be clear about what they do provide to students. If institutions aren't clear, or what you need to be successful is not provided by the institution or faculty members teaching the courses, then you should pursue other distance learning alternatives. Distance learning is here to stay, and many opportunities will continue to emerge for students who either prefer and/or require this educational option.

HEALTH AND WELLNESS: THERE IS A RELATIONSHIP TO COLLEGE SUCCESS

Setting goals, prioritizing roles, and ensuring that you have the academic and social support you need are important to succeeding in distance learning. However, if you haven't paid enough attention to issues of personal health and wellness, you risk not completing your courses because of illness. Each of us has developed a personal approach to health. Our primary recommendation is that you evaluate your approach and make adjustments as you see fit to help ensure that you remain healthy.

This is not a handbook about eating well and taking care of yourself. Since it is a guide to helping you succeed in learning, however, the topics of health and wellness are essential. *There is a relationship between being healthy and effective learning.* For example, it is clear that taking care of your body—eating well, exercising regularly, and getting sufficient rest—has a positive effect on your ability to concentrate and on your memory. Being healthy also affects your ability to effectively handle stress. (See Chapter 6 for more information about stress management.) Do we all do this? Probably not, but we should. Let's look at issues related to diet, exercise, rest, and leisure so that you can begin to evaluate your own approach to health and wellness.

 Worksheet #4, "Health & Wellness: A Short Self-Assessment and Plan for Change," has been developed to help guide you through the self-assessment questions asked in the next section. This worksheet is available on the Guide's Web site.

The Basics of Good Health: Diet, Exercise, and Rest

Diet.   Most of us already know about good nutrition, but we sometimes need to be reminded of it before we reach for that "study snack," which usually consists of a bag of chips, a bowl of popcorn, a soda, and perhaps even a handful of chocolate chip cookies. By themselves, and in moderation, these snacks are not necessarily going to be detrimental to your health and well-being. However, when they are coupled with the absence of a healthy breakfast and the grabbing of a "quick lunch" at the local burger palace—to be eaten while driving to your next meeting—they can pose a problem. So, we really ought to explore healthier ways of eating.

In brief, guidelines suggest that you should be:

- Eating a variety of foods.
- Maintaining a healthy weight.
- Choosing a diet low in fat, especially saturated fat, and cholesterol.
- Eating plenty of vegetables, fruits, and grains.
- Using sugar only in moderation.
- Using salt only in moderation.
- Drinking alcoholic beverages (if used) only in moderation.

A lot has been written about developing good eating habits. There are additional resources on our Web site to explore if you wish. For our purposes, it is more important that you determine how closely you want to follow these guidelines, and that you make the necessary adjustments to accomplish them. Do a self-assessment by asking yourself questions, such as the following. Use the space below or Worksheet #4 on the Web site to record your answers.

- Where is your diet relative to these guidelines?

- How satisfied are you with your current diet?

_____

_____

- What changes are you ready to make (if any) to come closer to your ideal diet?

_____

_____

_____

_____

Exercise. An effective exercise program does not have to involve expensive equipment and a lot of time. Participating in some type of aerobic exercise improves your body's functioning and thus your ability to concentrate and perform tasks more efficiently. There are many books and references, including videotapes, to help you develop an aerobic exercise plan that works for you. As always recommended, you should check with your own physician to help you design a plan that *works* for you, as opposed to one that may be detrimental to your health.

 As with diet, take the time to do a self-assessment. Here are some questions to ask yourself. Use the space below or Worksheet #4 on the Web site to record your answers.

- Do you have an exercise plan?

_____

- Are you satisfied with how you feel and your general sense of health?

_____

- What changes could or should be made to bring you closer to what you believe to be your optimum level of health?

_____

_____

_____

Rest. In the section on setting your role priorities, you were asked how much sleep you require to be at your best performance. You

were also asked when you were most alert and prepared to learn (morning, afternoon, evenings, or some combination). These questions assume that you require some level of rest to ensure that you are operating at your maximum effectiveness. The body needs time to rejuvenate itself—to relax and recuperate from the day's events and activities. However, it is common knowledge that each of us requires a different amount of sleep and rest. You need to pay attention to your body's need for rest. To ensure that you get the rest you need, build it into your priorities and daily time management plan. If you don't, you will find that you are neither doing justice to your health nor to your classes.

 Following are more questions for your self-assessment. Use the space below or Worksheet #4 on the Web site to record your answers.

- How much rest do you require?

_____

- Are you getting it? Why or why not?

_____

_____

- If you aren't getting enough rest, is it affecting your performance at work, school, or with your family?

_____

_____

- If so, how can you make changes to accommodate your need for additional rest?

_____

_____

Where Does Fun Fit into All This?

Remember the story about Cheryl who decided that her leisure time was something that she was unwilling to compromise as she pursued her college courses? For Cheryl, the small amount of time she allocated to leisure activities was essential for maintaining a healthy outlook on life.

What is leisure for one is not leisure for another. Leisure is often defined as recreation. Some use a more literal translation of recreation and talk about leisure as a way to re-create oneself. In this regard, leisure is defined in its broadest context and would include areas related to your psychological, physical, and intellectual self. In this context, some may view taking college courses as an activity they pursue for fun. Others may find course work stressful and look to other activities for their enjoyment. *What is your definition of leisure?* Use Worksheet #4 on the Web site to record your answers. However you define leisure, it is important to identify at least some time during the week for activities related to "having fun."

Handbooks developed to improve student success often include sections on health and being healthy. Issues related to health are included because they are important and, as stated earlier, there is a relationship between health and doing your best academically. If you are tired, your concentration is affected and, consequently, so is your ability to recall and retain information. The same is true if you are ill. While you may intuitively know that maintaining your health is important to doing well in your courses, you may not take the steps needed to ensure that you remain healthy. For example, in an already busy life with role commitments and responsibilities, it is often personal time—rest and leisure—that suffers. Sharon's experience in juggling her commitments and academic workload is how many of us manage to "get everything done": We just burn the proverbial candle at both ends, hoping the pain is short-lived.

A personal decision to change behaviors should be based on an evaluation of your current behaviors related to your health. What are your current practices and how do these relate to where you want to be? If there is a mismatch, then you can decide to make the changes necessary to achieve your desired level of health. The following questions can help you begin to make an initial assessment of your personal approach to health and wellness:

- **Diet:** Do you generally follow the guidelines noted in the diet section of this chapter?
- **Exercise:** Do you exercise regularly?
- **Rest:** Do you know how much rest you need to be at your best? Do you make sure that you get it?
- **Fun:** What do you define as leisure and how does it relate to your priorities?
- **Personality and health:** Do you have a positive outlook on life?

For each of these areas, determine your level of satisfaction with your current behavior, and then decide where you would like to be. Is there a mismatch? If so, you need to develop a plan for change. The resources on the Guide's companion Web site can help you learn more about health and wellness and develop strategies to help you achieve your desired goals.

SUMMARY: A FINAL NOTE

This chapter has attempted to identify those areas related to self that can serve as barriers to successful distance learning. Among the most important of these are unclear goals; interference of other commitments; lack of a system of support; and, finally, lack of attention to issues of health and wellness. All of these areas are personal and depend on one's own wants, needs, and priorities. At the end of each section, questions were listed as tools to help you make decisions about your priorities, your learning needs, and your personal health and wellness. The fundamental questions of this chapter include:

- What are your reasons for being a student?
- What are your role priorities and how does being a student fit within them?
- What kind of support do you need to be a successful student?
- What resources are available to you through the faculty member, other students, or the distance learning institution to meet your support needs?
- What is your assessment of your own health and wellness? If there is a mismatch between your reality and your ideal, how can you design a plan that will move you closer to your ideal?

If you understand your goals, set your priorities, identify your learning needs and actively seek to meet them, and take care of your health, you will be well on your way to solving those personal issues that can become barriers to your success in distance learning.

CHAPTER 6

IMPROVING DISTANCE LEARNING PERFORMANCE

Steps to Success

In this chapter you will

- ◆ find specific detailed guidance to help you succeed in your course of studies
- ◆ gain a new understanding of learning and studying
- ◆ learn that succeeding as a student means really learning how to learn and enjoying the learning
- ◆ learn how to make steady progress toward achieving your goal of a degree or certificate
- ◆ learn effective methods of studying, note taking, time management, stress management, reading, writing, and test taking

I t is critically important that you learn to improve your distance learning performance because, as a distance learner, you are more on your own than most classroom learners—consequently, you must take more responsibility for your own learning.

This chapter begins with general ideas about learning and then teaches specific techniques. If you are eager to look at the techniques before reading about the background ideas, jump right into the section "Study Guides." But be sure to return and read "Learning to Learn" because you need to know how and why specific techniques work if you are to modify them to best fit your own circumstances and learning style.

INTRODUCTION

Students who are new to distance learning are often concerned about how well they will be able to do in their courses and whether distance learning courses will be harder than traditional classroom courses. You've already learned, in Chapter 1, that there are many varieties of distance education that use different modalities. The first thing to recognize about this sprawling variety of distance learning courses is that you will find some delivery modes more appealing than others.

Try to find the mode of instruction that works best for you. Some people do well and prefer studying on their own, while others need the stimulation of interaction (introverts versus extroverts). Some people do best hearing material presented, while others learn better seeing material in books and videos (visual and auditory learners). Still others need to interact with the materials by drawing or moving objects (kinesthetic learners). Different learning styles match up well or poorly with different modes of instruction; try to learn about what works and doesn't work for you.

TIP

References for this chapter are available on our companion Web site. You will also find links to numerous how-to-study resources that are available online.

Whatever delivery medium is used in a course, you should take advantage of every opportunity to use all the available learning resources. As discussed in Chapter 5, use whatever way you can to make contact with your instructor, your advisor, your fellow students, and with learning support staff who can help you. The first basic guideline for becoming a more effective learner is this: Communicate early and often with whomever can be of help. Don't wait until you are doing poorly in a class before seeking help. By making contact early and letting people know who you are, you establish a learner–teacher relationship that will be available when you really need it.

Distance learning courses are generally as effective as traditional classroom courses, no matter what modality is used for instruction. If given a choice, of course, most students would prefer to take classes that involve direct contacts with the instructor and other students. Students usually choose distance education courses because of the convenience and flexibility of taking a class that does not require that they be at a certain place at a certain time. Distance learning students are generally more motivated to succeed in their studies and to learn effective techniques of learning and studying. So let's get started.

LEARNING TO LEARN

The phrase "learning to learn" appears frequently in how-to-study books, but this section is concerned with attitudes and ideas about learning rather than specific study techniques. It will be worthwhile to examine a few core facts and ideas about learning before getting into details about improving your studying. We'll be building on the learning skills that you already have. The object is to become more aware of what enters into the act of learning so that you can learn even more efficiently and effectively—and become more confident about what you are doing.

Learning more about how you learn is something like reading the manual for your computer. You can certainly use the computer without ever reading the user's manual, but you'll be better prepared to care for the computer, handle emergencies, and use applications more effectively and efficiently if you read the manual.

The second basic guideline for becoming a more effective learner is this: Always remember that all learning is to some extent self-learning and must be self-guided and self-motivated. The more you know about yourself as a learner, the better you will be at guiding your own learning. Even if you have the best teacher in the world sitting at your elbow in a tutorial setting, you will not learn, remember, and use what you learn if you do not put forth a conscious, well-informed effort.

Following are six interesting facts and ideas from the fields of psychology and education to orient your study of learning techniques.

Interesting Fact #1
Effective Learning Requires Active Organizing

Some of the best insights about how to learn come from looking at what has been written about helping teachers teach. Teachers are taught to organize course material into segments that can be ordered and assimilated. Unfortunately, the act of organizing for meaning is something that students often disregard and are not taught to do. Instead, students stay passive about their learning, while teachers do the active learning. Animal experiments have demonstrated that rats who are barged (or "shipped") through a water maze will not learn the route of the maze, while rats that swim the maze do learn the route. We've all experienced the difference between being driven to a place and not learning how to get there versus driving to a destination and learning the route.

Of course, students will use the organization already provided by the instructor and by their textbooks, but students *must* make the effort to be in the driver's seat and not be merely a passenger on a route chosen by the teacher. Being in the driver's seat means to actively reflect, to think, to question, and to consider alternative ways of doing or saying things. In other words, you must intend and plan to learn.

Interesting Fact #2
It Does Take Time to Assimilate New Learning

The three key processes in memory are typically described as encoding, storage, and retrieval. Encoding involves getting information into memory. Storage involves maintaining encoded information in memory over time. Retrieval involves recovering information from memory stores. The level of processing of information is closely related to how effectively it will be stored and retrieved. Shallow processing encodes nothing more than the physical structure or a stimulus: Is a word written in CAPITAL letters? Intermediate processing emphasizes the sound of a word: Does a word rhyme with "bee"? Deep processing emphasizes the meaning of a word: Would the word fit in the sentence "He met a _____ on the street"?

Studying will be most effective when it involves deep processing for meaning rather than shallow processing.

What About Cramming?

Should you ever "cram" for your studies? Well, the "should" hardly matters because you undoubtedly will be in a position at some point when you just haven't had enough time to study adequately and will need to cram as much learning as possible in a very short time. Spaced learning over time has been shown to be the most effective for promoting deep encoding, long storage, and good retrieval. There is no denying, however, that cramming can work to quickly cram in learning when that material does not need to be retained for a long time. Although you may need to cram occasionally, try to avoid doing it as a regular practice if you want to optimize your long-term learning. Recent research has shown that, at the biochemical level, the production of new proteins in the brain is required for memories to become permanent. Such production takes time.

Interesting Fact #3
Feelings Are Important in Remembering

If you doubt that feelings are important for remembering, just think about the last time you had a strong emotional experience, such as a near miss in an automobile collision, an accident, or an angry encounter. We usually can remember such incidents clearly with vivid recall of what happened just before, during, and after the emotional event. Indeed, sometimes the problem is how to stop remembering traumatic events that can interfere with our everyday lives if they persist as intrusive memories.

A less dramatic but more pervasive illustration of the role of emotion in memory is found in the familiar "tip-of-the-tongue" phenomenon. That happens when we are sure that we know the answer to some question, such as the name of a person or place, but can't recall (retrieve) what we are sure that we know. Most of us will experience this phenomenon about once a week, but its incidence does increase with age. Numerous research studies have shown that when we feel that we know something, the odds are that we do indeed know the fact or place name or person's name that we can't immediately produce. Given more time or hints, or if asked to choose the correct answer from among a number of similar but wrong answers, we are very likely to come up with the correct answer. Feelings can be an accurate guide to what we know and don't know and to what we can remember or not remember.

One reason why students should always try to be active in their learning rather than passive is because active learning provides more feeling cues than passive learning. It is sometimes difficult to get excited about material that we must learn when we don't find the material intrinsically interesting. You will generate just the right level of feeling compatible with learning if you try to answer questions when studying or note taking, rather than merely reading or listening. A helpful tension will be created when you pose a question for which you do not yet have the answer.

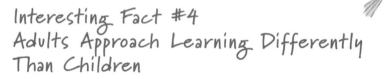

Interesting Fact #4
Adults Approach Learning Differently Than Children

The age-old belief that adults are more limited than children in the ability to learn new things is false. The "old dogs can't learn new tricks theory" was disproved early in the history of experimental psychology. In 1928, pioneering educational psychologist Edward Thorndike wrote that "adults can learn rather easily and rapidly, and probably could learn much more than they do." He went on to say, "Adults learn much less than they might partly because they underestimate their power of learning, and partly because of unpleasant attention and comment . . . [and] adults learn less than they might because they do not care enough about learning." Thus if you are apprehensive about your ability to succeed in adult distance education courses, remember: You can do this!

Although adults are able to learn most things as quickly and effectively as children, there are differences in the ways that children and adults approach learning. The basic notion is that adults are more self-guided in their learning than children. Due to their wider experience, adults can bring more to the learning task than children can bring, and adults can take away more to apply to their everyday lives.

It is essential that adult learning be learner-centered, because adults will not do many tasks just because "the teacher said to do it." For adults, learning needs to make sense. Consequently, if you do not find the material in your course inherently interesting, then you need to work to add value and interest to the subject for yourself.

Interesting Fact #5
There Are Different Ways of Being Smart

For many years, the theory of "general intelligence" dominated the fields of psychology and education. You took an intelligence test and got one score that labeled you as smart or dumb or normal. In the last two or three decades, psychologists have been more disposed to think of "multiple intelligences" and to believe that there are different dimensions of being intelligent. Harvard psychologist Howard Gardner has identified the following eight distinct intelligences:

- Visual-spatial learners think in terms of physical space. They are comfortable with models, graphics, charts, and drawings.
- Bodily-kinesthetic learners have a keen sense of body awareness and learn well through physical activity and role-playing.
- Musical learners are sensitive to rhythm and sound. They may study better with music in the background.
- Intrapersonal learners understand themselves well but may shy away from others. They can be taught through independent study and introspection.
- Interpersonal learners relate well to others, noticing moods, motivations, and feelings. They can learn through cooperative learning and teamwork.
- Linguistic learners use words effectively. They like reading, playing word games, or making up poetry or stories.
- Logical-mathematical learners think conceptually, and abstractly, and they are able to see and explore patterns and relationships.
- Naturalistic learners understand their environment. They are interested in ecological balance and may study better in natural surroundings.

These different intelligences, strengths, or competencies may each have its own developmental history. In other words, it would be possible for a person to be very advanced in one competency at an early age (say musical intelligence) but not attain much competency in another intelligence (say interpersonal intelligence) until a much later age. The most valuable insight for adults is that lifelong learning can be thought of not just as the continuing effort to learn new content and skills but as the lifelong development of our own multiple intelligences. We aren't stuck with just being "not musical," "not mathematical," "not word-minded," "not artistic," or "not athletic." We can recognize that some of our competencies emerge much earlier or much later than others did.

The multiple-intelligences approach can be applied directly to the educational setting. You can recognize that any course or subject matter will engage different intelligences, and that you bring more development to one subject than to others. You must give yourself basic help in some subjects, while other subjects will be easy because they call upon competencies that you've already developed.

Interesting Fact #6
Some Schools Fit Some Students
Better Than Others

Extensive educational research has shown that how well students do in school depends on the school–student fit. Students who do mediocre work in one college may do very well in another; not because one college is easier than the other, but because there is a better fit of student to college in the second institution. This fit helps the student to become involved with the institution rather than staying uninvolved. Keep this fact in mind when you explore distance learning institutions. You need to find a college or university that fits you, instead of trying to fit yourself into the mold of the institution. You need to become involved in working with the faculty, the staff, your advisors, and with other students at the place that you choose. To repeat some earlier advice: You may wish to take a class or two to see if you are comfortable with distance education and the style of the instructors and advisors at the school.

If you are like most distance learning students, you will be reentering higher education rather than starting college for the first time. Adult students are often self-conscious about their status as reentry students and frequently feel inferior to students who persisted in their degree efforts without dropping out. However, statistics show that of every 100 entrants to higher education only about 45 eventually will obtain a bachelor's degree (another 13 to 14 will earn an associate's degree). These statistics mean that students who succeed are in the *minority.* The majority, 55 percent, drop out and stay out. By returning to college as an adult, you are taking the first step to putting yourself among the minority of students who eventually will succeed. Stopping out for a time is different than dropping out and staying out. Among students who leave college, nearly 30 percent do reenroll.

Other research has shown that it is the quality of the student's effort that predicts success in college rather than fixed factors such as parental education, race, age, and gender. When a student commits to doing well and puts forth a quality effort, then that student is likely to succeed. Various theories have been propounded about how college helps students to change. They all focus on the college–student fit, which will facilitate student involvement with her own education and with the educators at the institution.

STUDY GUIDES

Now that you have an overview about learning to learn, let's get into the particulars of how-to-study techniques. Every student who enters or reenters college would benefit from spending some time reading about study techniques. Those who already are good students will learn a few new tricks. Those who aren't can learn the mechanics that contribute to being a good student.

This chapter is intended to provide a general orientation to becoming a better distance learner and specific recommendations about techniques to apply. You will find more than enough suggestions to get you started in your new study efforts. There are numerous other study guides to help you discover the ideas and techniques that work best for you. There also are a number of study aids available online, many of which can be found at the Guide's Web site.

Most guidebooks include coverage not only of study techniques but also of time management, reading, note taking, writing papers, taking tests, and all the other activities that enter into being an effective student. However, few guidebooks are directed at adult students who are taking courses and attempting to complete their degrees via distance learning (like this Guide). Therefore, it will be necessary for you to adapt some of these study recommendations into steps that you can apply in distance learning courses. Whichever study guide you read, make sure to apply the techniques promptly to your course. It does no good to just read about studying more effectively. You must put the techniques to work.

The SQ4R Study Method

The reliable, much-used SQ4R method has been described in innumerable study guides. SQ4R means "Scan, Question, Read, Recite (or Rite), Recall, and Review." As a technique, it manages to capture much (but not everything) about being an active learner rather than a passive learner. Imagine that you are in a typical course with typical expectations. Your assignment is to read the first two chapters of the assigned textbook in week one of the course and be prepared to take a quiz the following week.

Here's how you would apply the SQ4R method:

- **Scan or Survey.** Don't begin by reading the first assigned chapter. Instead scan or survey it. By surveying a chapter, you get an overview and gain some familiarity with the main terms and phrases. You are reading to see *how* the chapter is organized rather than trying to understand *what* is said. Don't read word for word, just scan. If the author provides an outline or a summary, do read that more carefully.

- **Question.** Go back over the chapter and formulate questions based on the parts or sections that you've identified as important. The author may have provided questions at the end of the chapter for you, but it is essential that you *make up your own questions based upon how you first see the chapter.* You will be revising your questions (and your answers) as you read the chapter more carefully, so don't worry about developing precise, complete questions on the first pass.

- **Read.** Now that you've formulated your questions, read the chapter carefully and purposefully to answer the questions that you identified. As you read, you may find that you want to reword some of your questions and perhaps add questions that you had overlooked in your first survey. (We'll say more about types of reading in the section on reading guides.) The key to effective reading is to read for understanding. The self-guided test of your understanding is whether you can answer your own questions.

- **Recite or Rite.** The key in this step is to use your own words to answer your questions based upon the reading that you just did. You *must* answer in your own words rather than merely repeating what you read, but be careful that you don't inadvertently change the meaning of the question or the author's points. Don't write too much, just enough to sketch your answers. Pretend that you're taking an exam and answer in the way that you know will be required in the course. If you will be writing short essay exams, then make your answers that length; if you will be taking multiple-choice tests, then make your answers shorter.

- **Recall.** When you recall, you are practicing to remember. Go back through the questions and, without looking at your notes or written answers, come up with the answer again. Leave a little time between the recite step and the recall step, so that you can truly see if you remember enough to produce the answer.

- **Review.** Reviewing depends on timing. In this step, you would go on to read and apply the SQ4R method to the second chapter before undertaking your review. You must decide when to review your questions and again recall your answers, depending on the exam schedule for the course. If you will be tested on the assigned materials weekly, then you must review weekly; if you will only be taking a midterm and a final, then you need to review in several staggered sessions before those exams. Do not try to apply the entire SQ4R method just before an exam. Reviewing is dependent on completion of the previous steps; you can't review what you haven't given yourself time to study.

Exercise 6.1

Take 15 minutes to apply this simple study method to this chapter by doing the first two steps. You've already read to this point, but start over again by scanning the entire chapter then making up some questions based on what you see as the most important ideas of the chapter. Come back to this point when you are done surveying and formulating questions. You'll have a much different perspective on what is being said than you would if you had simply read it straight through and done nothing else.

Concept (or Mental) Mapping

To learn effectively, you must take control of your own learning. The way to do that is to become a teacher to yourself, for yourself, and, if necessary, by yourself. By thinking like a teacher when you approach a learning task, you will be putting yourself in the most advantageous position for learning. Your full role as a learner is to be a teacher, your own teacher, for your own learning.

Every adult who is reading these words already is a successful learner at a number of tasks. Although you may not have been very successful at academic learning previously, think about something that you do well. Perhaps it is a sport, cooking, music, something artistic, or something at your work. Undoubtedly, this activity required a learning period that lasted for years, during which you acquired a set of skills. You also gained a mental map of how to do what you do. Now, you must learn to form a mental map, or concept map, for every academic course that you take; just as you successfully formed a mental map for everything you already know how to do well.

All of us construct and use mental maps each day. The most common experience of mental mapping is when we travel to a different section of a city. At first, everything looks unfamiliar; we have no detailed mental map at all. Our first "map" is like the old maps of the New World in the days of Columbus, where everything beyond a certain border was labeled "Unknown." Pointing to the unknown *is* a kind of map because at least we know where the unknown begins. As we traverse an area, certain landmarks emerge, and our mental map becomes more elaborate, perhaps by adding a street name, a church spire, or a gas station. If we travel the route often, the mental map becomes very elaborate, so that we can actually anticipate what we will see along the route. Interestingly, even elaborate mental maps are likely to have gaps because we don't learn what is around every corner in every direction. We learn only what we need to reach our destination. Another interesting fact is that different people have very different mental maps, although they are all able to reach a given destination. This is because the features that are important in one person's map are not important in another person's.

Sports provide an instructive example concerning mental maps. A number of research studies have demonstrated that it is *more* effective to divide practice time for a sport into mental practice *and* physical practice than to spend all the time in one or the other. It is just as important to visualize the sequence of movements involved in performing a basketball free throw—to imagine the sequence of sensations and positions to be executed—as it is to actually practice free throws. Without a clear mental picture of what to do, an aspiring athlete will introduce variations in the movement, so the pattern cannot be reliably repeated.

The point of this discussion about mental, or concept, maps is *that a fundamental part of learning must be focused on the construction of a concept map for any subject that is being studied and for all the parts of the subject.* Without developing a concept map that becomes increasingly detailed and interconnected, students are simply memorizing. Even memorizing is almost impossible without constructing some learning plan. It is possible to apply the SQ4R method as a drill and to overlook the need to couple it with concept mapping. When a study method is coupled with a conscious effort to form concept maps, however, learning becomes powerful and efficient.

Of course, the map is not the actual place. Maps are abstract representations of places. Similarly, the map of a subject or course is not the course. If you memorize the map, you will not have learned the course; but the map does help guide your learning in the course. Using someone else's map can be helpful, but what is *most* valuable in learning is constructing your own map. With your map, you are traveling through the subject as a newcomer and not an expert. The expert's map will be too detailed and too layered for the beginner.

The Value of Doodling.   The easiest way to get started with concept mapping in your studies is to indulge in the common art of doodling. As soon as you approach a course, a book, or an assignment be sure to have plenty of "doodle paper" at hand so that you can simply draw connections between words, ideas, and methods as you read. Don't try to be artistic or produce engineering diagrams, just doodle. You will throw away most of your doodles, but you may end up with a few that so clearly map what you've been reading or hearing that you will want to keep them to guide you in further studies and pre-exam reviews. (If you plan to become president of the United States, please keep *all* your doodles in a safe-deposit box because they will be worth a lot of money to your heirs, like John F. Kennedy's famous doodles.)

The kind of doodling described here is very different from the doodling that you might do when you pay no attention to what you are reading or hearing. Study doodling helps you to organize and identify important points. Drawing cartoons or sketch doodling is just a way to avoid boredom.

Exercise 6.2

Try doodling right now. Take a sheet of paper and draw some lines, arrows, boxes, triangles, circles, question marks, exclamation points, and other figures that connect the different words and ideas that you've been reading in this section on study guides; print the **WORDS** and **IDEAS** in big, bold print. Remember that the purpose of your doodles is to represent the mental map that you are developing. It is fine if there are places where the doodles show that you do not know what connects with what or what leads to what—by knowing that you don't know, you'll be preparing yourself to learn more. Doodles are visual statements and visual question marks. Study doodling provides an easy preliminary way to organize and map what you are trying to learn.

The "I CARE" System.   Professors Bob Hoffman and Donn Ritchie of San Diego State University have been working with instructors in the California State University system to help them create online courses. The core idea is that both students and instructors benefit by having a mental model of their course. Each module of their online workshop is organized around what they call the "I CARE" five-step system——Introduction, Connect, Apply, Reflect, and Extend.

- The *introduction* places the module in the context of the course as a whole.

- The *connect* section presents new information in context by using charts, diagrams, illustrations, or other tools to map the new information to the other parts of the course, that is, what came before in other modules and what will follow.

- *Apply* is the practice section of the module, which is using the information and concepts in the module.

- The *reflect* section asks students to reflect on what they've just learned—from responding to questions from the instructor, to journal entries, to peer exchanges, or other reflective activities.

- Finally, *extend* is where more is added to what was done in that module. It uses everything from evaluating what was presented and how meaningful/useful/interesting it was to providing additional resources.

Distance learning students may apply the I CARE system to their own learning. The way to do that is to take the books, assignments, syllabi, lecture notes, tapes, software, and other resources available to you and attempt to actively organize those materials in the same way that you would if you were an instructor. The difference between the way you undertake this activity and the way an instructor would do it is that you apply the I CARE system after you've looked at the organization and materials. Your instructor will have drawn on years of experience to organize the course, which allows you to draw on the instructor's organization.

As you can see, this is a much more sophisticated and demanding activity than simply applying the SQ4R method to assignments, but the two activities do overlap. Think of the SQ4R method as the "micromethod" to use when studying a specific assignment and the I CARE system as the "macromethod" to apply to the course as a whole. By using both, you will be working on the details that must be mastered for succeeding in a course and the big picture and framework that you must construct if you are to be successful at long-term learning.

Concept mapping is a way to think about what you are doing when you apply the I CARE system. Doodling is an activity that can be applied on your way to developing more elaborate concept maps. If you are reading a textbook that is well organized and listening to lectures that are interestingly presented and well linked to the text and the syllabus, then you've already been given the major framework, which you can simply improve for yourself by using the I CARE method. If the materials are more scattered, then you will need to do more work to organize them. To be an effective learner, you must make the effort to develop your own concept maps. Without that effort, you will never be in control of your own learning.

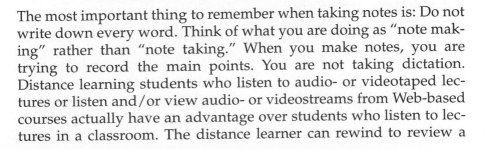

NOTE TAKING

The most important thing to remember when taking notes is: Do not write down every word. Think of what you are doing as "note making" rather than "note taking." When you make notes, you are trying to record the main points. You are not taking dictation. Distance learning students who listen to audio- or videotaped lectures or listen and/or view audio- or videostreams from Web-based courses actually have an advantage over students who listen to lectures in a classroom. The distance learner can rewind to review a section of the lecture that wasn't clear. The disadvantage for distance learning students is that you can't ask questions during or just after the lecture. To overcome this disadvantage and to avoid listening passively, imagine that you are listening to the lecture live, and pretend that you can ask any question at any time. Always write your questions among your notes, and take the first opportunity to look for answers in the text or handouts. If you can't find answers that clarify the lectures from print resources, then be sure to communicate with the instructor by whatever means you have (email, fax, telephone, etc.).

Five-Stage Note Taking

A popular technique for taking notes is the five-stage Cornell System developed by Walter Pauk. The five stages are Record, Reduce, Recite, Reflect, and Review (you will notice some overlap with the SQ4R study method).

- **Record.** Draw a vertical line from the top to the bottom of a page (use enough pages to cover the lecture). The left column will be your recall column. Leave it blank until after the lecture. During the lecture, your emphasis is on active listening. In the right column, record and sketch as much information as you believe is important while listening to the lecture. Use an outline or doodle concept map form. Write down exactly what the instructor is saying only if he indicates that it is important to get a sentence or phrase precisely. Always do the prereading that is recommended before the lecture. Then you will know what you do not need to include in your notes because you already have notes from your SQ4R studying. Write your notes in "telegraphese" rather than complete sentences and use sentence phrases and word outlines, which would not be acceptable for a formal essay. Remember, you are the only one who needs to understand your notes.

- **Reduce.** As soon after the lecture as you can, condense your notes into a few words, abbreviations, or phrases in the left recall column. In effect you are preparing prompt cards on the left column, using just a few words or phrases that will jog your memory of the original lecture.

- **Recite.** In this stage, try to cover your notes and say what is in them in your own words. You are giving a minilecture or summary of the original lecture. If you need prompts, look at the words or phrases that are on the left side. After you go through the recitation, uncover your notes and check yourself for completeness and accuracy.

- **Reflect.** Allow a few days to pass before doing this stage. Then, reread your notes and think about how they relate to your reading and to lectures that preceded or followed this one. You may want to modify or correct your notes based upon your expanded understanding.

- **Review.** In this stage you do *spaced* reviews of all your accumulated notes over the weeks of the term; as you are reviewing, continue to annotate and modify your original notes so that they become more elaborated and more organized.

Although doodling is not a part of the Cornell System, you can use additional sheets to add concept-mapping doodles to your lecture notes, especially in the reflect and review stages.

TIME AND STRESS MANAGEMENT

As discussed in Chapter 5, there are no time management secrets that will allow you to convert 24 hours in a day into 48 hours. So, the first thing to do in managing your time is to *realistically* evaluate how much time you have for studying. The general rule is to allow two to three hours of outside study time per week for each credit of a course. For a five-credit course you should study 10 to 15 hours a week, in addition to whatever time you put in on distance learning "class attendance." *Don't sign up for more hours of course work than you can handle.* Adult students who are working full time and involved in family and community responsibilities should not try to carry the same number of credit hours as an 18- to 25-year-old on-campus student who is not working. It's impossible!

Some students returning to college are advised to take no more than one or two classes in their first term. In this way, they can succeed at their first courses. They also learn how much time they have available and how much they need for studying (see Chapter 5 for a discussion of balancing study and other responsibilities). This advice may prompt you to say, "But I'll never finish. I'll never get my degree." Not true! You will be able to finish, and you will be able to add more courses per term once you devise a study schedule and develop a study routine. A sure way to never complete your degree is to fail your first courses. Start a pattern of success and you will continue to succeed as a student. Start a pattern of failure and you will be likely to drop out.

Most traditional students study far too little and are then puzzled when they fail or do poorly in classes, and they are dismayed when they drop out. Recent results from the UCLA Higher Education Research Institute's annual survey of college first-year students show that 66 percent spent less than six hours per week studying (this includes reading, reviewing notes, writing papers, doing research, etc.). One reason traditional students sometimes view adult students as "grade busters" is because adults who are returning to school realize that they must put in study time to do well. If you manage your time so that you study two to three hours outside class for every credit hour that you take and do not sign up for too many credit hours, you undoubtedly will do better in your courses than students who do not acknowledge that studying takes time.

The Lakein ABC Method of Time Management

The essence of the time management method developed by Allan Lakein is to list, prioritize, and check. First, list the jobs or tasks that you know you need to do during the coming week. The order of the list makes no difference, simply make the list. You can add to the list during the week if other things come up or if you find that you overlooked something important.

Next, review your list of miscellaneous learning tasks and prioritize it by assigning an **A**, a **B**, or a **C** to the left of each item. An **A** item is one that you must complete during the week; a **B** item is one that you want to accomplish during the week; a **C** item is one that you know you need to do eventually but is not necessary to finish that week. (The time scale can be changed if doing daily, or bi-weekly, or monthly lists works better for you, but it is best to start with making a weekly list and modifying the time scale later.)

Examine the list before you to attempt to prioritize it. If you have all **A**'s, something is very wrong, you are trying to put out fires all week long! Similarly, if you have all **C**'s, you may want to reexamine your priorities because not many students can let their studies slide for an entire week without getting something done. To do well with time management, you must learn to discriminate what needs to be done immediately from what can wait until later.

Now try to apply your list for a week. Review the list each morning to see what you must do and what must be given priority. Each time that you complete a task, check it off with a large colored check mark (✔). You'll find that you enjoy checking off items. At the end of the week, you need to study what you've done. If you don't have all your **A** items checked off, you need to change the way that you schedule your study time; you must reserve time to do the **A**'s first. If you find that you have little or nothing checked off, you need to reconsider whether you are committed to meeting your goals as a student.

Sustained procrastination can be an indication that psychological problems are of more pressing concern than schoolwork. Procrastination is an almost irresistible subject for jokes. (Have you heard the one about the Procrastinators Club meeting announcement: Come Whenever You Get Around to It?) For some individuals, procrastination is not a joke. It is a serious problem that requires counseling.

For most students, special help will not be needed. With a little practice, you will be able to use the Lakein ABC method to set up your learning jobs every week and adjust the time that you need to allocate for studying depending on the mix of **A**s, **B**s, and **C**s that you have each week. You can modify the Lakein method by adding columns or pages for work activities and one for home or recreation activities.

The reality is that anything that you do not list as an **A**, **B**, or **C** activity automatically becomes a **D** activity—a default—something that you consider so unimportant that it is not even listed among your priorities. Do not wait to make your home or recreation list until you have finished all of your school and work activities. If you do, then home or play becomes a **D** activity. You could get straight A's at school and flunk out at home.

Good Time Management Is Also Good Stress Management

You cannot be effective in juggling the tasks involved in the many roles that you have, as student, worker, parent, housekeeper, citizen, spouse, and so forth if you don't consciously make time for every-thing that is important in your life. (See Chapter 5 for more help with balancing your multiple roles.)

The basic difference between people who are happy and those who are not is the balance of positives and negatives that people have in their lives. Happier people have more positives and fewer nega-tives. Stress management depends on building up a robust ratio of positives to negatives, so that when negatives inadvertently enter your life, there still is a buffer of positives to offset the negatives. This means that it is essential to include in your weekly listing of activities a number of guaranteed positives. In that way, you take control of your own happiness. It also is essential to add new positives to your life when new negatives enter it. Don't just wait for the negatives to go away to return to "normal."

Stress management has shown that meaningfulness is one of the most powerful dimensions of personal life that can provide resistance to stress. People who feel that their lives are meaning-ful, in a way that contributes something to life more significant than their own ego needs, are able to withstand extremely stress-ful negatives. In a small but important way, you can contribute to the meaningfulness of your life as a student by becoming a learn-er who seeks meanings from your studies beyond performing well on examinations. Include enough time for activities that enlarge your role as a learner. Be sure to include tasks that take you beyond the assigned material into your own explorations as a learner.

THE STUDENT STRESSOR TEST

There is no doubt that being a student can be stressful, and adult reentry stu-dents can be exposed to considerable stress from many directions. It is healthy to pay attention to your stress level and to get help if you are experi-encing excessive stress for a period of months. The Hart Student Stressor Test can be a useful self-screening device to detect if students are carrying undue amounts of stress as they try to perform in their courses.

Try taking it now and see how you score. Take the test again next term. If you score above the 90th percentile, and if your score stays there for sev-eral terms, you should definitely seek professional help.

(continued)

Instructions: Rate the following items using a **1, 2, 3, 4, 5** scale, with **1** the anchor rating for "no stress," and **5** the anchor rating for an item that causes you "extreme stress." Be sure to rate every item.

_____ 1. Personal appearance.

_____ 2. Weight problems.

_____ 3. Fear of war.

_____ 4. Marital plans.

_____ 5. Living arrangements.

_____ 6. Problems with boyfriend/girlfriend/spouse.

_____ 7. Personal problems with your immediate family.

_____ 8. Drug/alcohol problems.

_____ 9. Financial concerns (e.g., tuition, housing).

_____ 10. Lack of close friends.

_____ 11. Child-care concerns.

_____ 12. Pressures at work.

_____ 13. Lack of personal time for yourself.

_____ 14. Current job-searching plans.

_____ 15. Car/transportation problems.

_____ 16. Membership in campus organizations.

_____ 17. Speaking in public.

_____ 18. Test anxiety (exams and finals).

_____ 19. Difficulty in class scheduling when starting new terms.

_____ 20. Competition with other students and peer groups.

_____ 21. Grades.

_____ 22. Difficulties with an instructor.

_____ 23. Postgraduate plans.

_____ 24. My overall level of physical health now is 1, very good—no problems, to 5, very poor—many physical difficulties.

_____ 25. My overall stress level right now in my life is 1, very low, to 5, very high.

Scoring: Add your ratings for items #1 through #23. A score of 48 is average, placing you at the 50th percentile for students in the normative group. A score of 40 is at the 25th percentile; 56 is the 75th percentile; and 66 is the 90th percentile and may indicate serious stress problems if it persists. Also, pay attention to your scores on items #24 and #25. If either one is rated 5, you may still be at risk even if your overall score on the Student Stressor Test is not high.

READING GUIDES

Mortimer Adler, philosopher and Great Books Program founder, distinguished between reading for information and reading for understanding. He identified four levels of reading as *elementary reading, inspectional reading, analytical reading,* and *syntopical reading.* Someone who is just trying to comprehend the words in a book is at the *elementary reading* level; *inspectional reading* is skimming or scanning; *analytical reading* is the reading that most students are attempting most of the time with textbooks; and *syntopical reading* is an advanced form of reading that must be done when critiquing a book or developing a thesis or paper that draws from several books.

Adler identified what he called *the essence of active reading* in four basic questions that a reader asks and tries to answer for expository or nonfiction works:

1. What is the book about as a whole? (Identify the leading theme of the book and the essential subordinate themes or topics.)
2. What is being said in detail and how? (Discover the author's main ideas, assertions, and arguments.)
3. Is the book true in whole or part? (Make some effort to evaluate whether the author's views are true.)
4. What of it? (What difference does the information or understanding that you obtain from the book make to you, and why does the author believe it is important?)

Adler believes these four questions "summarize the whole obligation of the reader. They apply to anything worth reading—a book or an article or even an advertisement" (Adler, p. 48).

Adler's questions may seem rather lofty and removed from the kind of reading tasks that most students undertake when they attempt to study a textbook. Most students never ask the third and fourth questions. They certainly are beyond what is ordinarily applied in the SQ4R study method presented earlier. However, reading that gets you through lower-division, introductory courses is not the kind of reading that will be necessary in advanced courses that require you to perform your own research and synthesize information and ideas from several sources. All too often, students restrict their reading to textbook reading and do not know how to read in a wider, deeper way. It is very important to learn to read at many levels and to recognize that there is a more advanced level of reading than what is required to simply read well enough from texts to pass exams.

Real education will continue for a lifetime, and you are likely to read more than textbooks after you leave college. Students need to understand that textbooks are compilations of information and ideas from primary sources. Primary sources are articles, chapters, monographs, and books that are not organized in the way that textbooks are usually organized. Students are advised to consult at least one additional textbook (and preferably several) beyond the text that is assigned for the course. Students are often astounded to learn that what one textbook author presents as the core of a subject is not even mentioned by a different author. Both authors are supposedly presenting the "same subject."

TIP Reading and questioning will be become second nature if you make up your own shorthand set of symbols for the margins of your books or on stick-on notes for library books. Such symbols are especially helpful if you need to do book reviews since they can be assembled into a rough draft.

WRITING PAPERS

All good writing is usually rewriting! Students sometimes believe that they should write perfect and complete papers on their first drafts, but that is not realistic. Unfortunately, this approach to writing is perpetuated because students are exposed in high school mostly to timed, short essay exams for which they need to write a good draft on their one and only attempt. But even in exam situations, you should leave a little time before you start writing to map out what you will say and in what order. Leave a little time at the end to proofread what you've written for spelling, grammar, and meaningfulness.

The blank page often intimidates poor writers, just as empty pots and pans and a refrigerator full of groceries would intimidate inexperienced cooks. But writing is easier than cooking. You can fill a page with doodles to get started, expand the doodles into a concept map, expand that into an outline, and then do a first draft that can be revised repeatedly. It is very difficult to make a poorly cooked omelet better, but you can convert poor writing into good writing with enough revisions. Some people view writing a book as an impossible task, an act of genius. They see a 300-page book as 300 blank pages that had to be filled in word by word, line by line without stopping from beginning to end. Of course, 300-page books are written just like 300-mile journeys are walked—step by step, with a mental map of what it takes to get from one place to another. The same people who are overwhelmed and intimidated by blank pages may be able to take an auto engine apart and put it back together, or navigate a plane trip, or cook a five-course meal for 40 people without hesitation.

The same skills that are involved in effective reading are useful for effective writing. Indeed, it is impossible to be a fine writer without being an accomplished reader. That's because you must learn to appreciate good writing as a reader before you can effectively criticize your own writing and guide your rewrites. One reason that few students begin college as effective writers is because very few are effective readers at the syntopical level.

TIP A recommendation for aspiring writers is to keep a folder of excerpts from writers that you admire. Make it an eclectic collection, including everything from newspaper articles to comic book dialogues to screenplays to textbook samples. Once you have a few models, you can pick one that comes closest to the writing task that you need to accomplish, and then measure whatever you write against the model that you've chosen. You gradually will internalize the model, and you'll no longer need to have it at hand when you write.

Let's consider the practical steps that are involved when you are fulfilling a typical writing assignment. Imagine that you need to write a 10- to 15-page midterm exam for an upper-division course. What do you need to do? Here are some suggestions:

1. First, carefully study the way the instructor has described the assignment. Don't write a paper that doesn't cover what the instructor asked for. For example: An instruction to "summarize and compare the theories of learning that are covered in your textbook" is quite different than an instruction to "summarize and compare the theories of learning that were extant in the 1940s in the field of psychology." You will need to go to the library and collect some resources about psychology in the 1940s to fulfill the second assignment; doing the first assignment just involves careful analytical reading of your textbook. Similarly, an instruction to "summarize and compare" is quite different than an instruction to "compare and speculate about the importance" of different theories of learning.

Your instructor may also give you specific guidelines about the format you should use for references, footnotes, and citations. If not, be sure to pick your own style and stay with it, don't skip from one format to another.

2. Apply the skill you now know from studying and reading—doodling. You will write better if you start putting things on paper, and your first jottings do not need to be complete sentences in complete paragraphs.

3. Compile the resources that you will draw on in your writing. These may include lecture notes, reading notes, articles, chapters, books—anything that you can use either to think about the subject or that will provide facts and quotes.

4. Begin to sketch an outline. Your outline just puts into words your doodle map. Don't worry if the outline is very sketchy at first. It has to be. Those elaborate outlines that you sometimes see in textbooks were written *after* the book was drafted, not *before*.

5. Begin to write the rough draft of the paper, and try to find a "voice" that works to convey your thoughts and meet the instructions of the assignment. Finding the voice is as important as finding the main points that you will express. For example, an informal, first-person voice may not work at all for some assignments ("I think Newton's first law is cool.") but will fit very well for other assignments (e.g., the classic high school English assignment to "tell about your summer vacation").

6. Push the rough draft to completion. At this stage, you are trying to get from the beginning through the middle and to the end of the paper. Don't worry now about logic, grammar, spelling, and punctuation. You are concerned with bulk production. Your goal now is to get a first product that can then be revised—and revised again.

TIP

Some writers do very long first drafts and then cut back; others do very brief first drafts and then expand. If your first draft of a 15-page paper turns out to be 30 pages long, that's fine; if it's 3 pages long, that's fine, too. Do whatever works for you!

7. Put your rough draft aside for at least several hours before attempting a revision. You want to return to the draft with fresh eyes and fresh ideas.

8. Go through the rough draft and begin to correct it for logic, spelling, punctuation, and grammar. Feel free to move sections and make notes where you need to add new sections. Be bold and delete

what doesn't seem to fit or make sense. (There's an old saying that a writer's best friend is a large wastebasket.) However, do keep copies of your original versions so that you can go back and retrieve something that you cut should you later decide that it can be used.

9. Prepare the second draft, again pushing through to completion. If you get stuck revising a certain section, make a note in the margin to return to it later; don't get stalled.

10. Again, put the draft aside and return to it later before you attempt to rewrite.

11. Now you're ready for the final draft. In this draft, you must finish everything, even difficult sections that were left incomplete in the second draft. For most school papers, three drafts will be sufficient; for special papers like senior capstones or theses, you may need to do more than three.

TIP Before you do the writing of the final draft, apply the SQ4R and I CARE methods to your own writing. Does it make sense? Would someone who reads what you've written learn something? Have you organized what you want to convey into sections that make it easy for the reader? Have you been an effective teacher for the reader? As you rewrite for the final draft, keep the reader in mind. You are not writing just for yourself; you are writing a paper that the instructor will read and that other students may read.

12. You are not done, even when you complete step eleven. You still need to proofread what you consider a final draft. Be sure to use all the tools that may be built into your word processor.

TIP If your word processor has a spell checker, be sure to use it, and use a dictionary when you are not sure if a word should be changed. Your word processor may also include an outliner, which will let you see what your chapter looks like in full sentence outline form; that's a good tool to use to examine the logical structure of your paper. Some word processors include a thesaurus function, so you can look for alternate words if you notice that you are repeating the same word too frequently. Many word processors also have a grammar checker; use that too, but use it cautiously because grammar checkers are not as accurate as spell checkers, and you need to know a good deal about grammar to decide if a recommended change is desirable. Never make a change just because the grammar checker suggests it; understand what is being suggested.

13. After all this work, be sure to print a copy of your paper with adequate margins and clear, clean printing. Always keep a copy for yourself; originals do get lost, so you need both an electronic and a print backup.

These 13 steps to good writing will not make you into a Hemingway or a Shakespeare, but they will give you a basis for writing that can be used again and again in your course work. Be sure to continue your explorations of writing by consulting the online resources that are available at the Web site. The Web links contain everything from style guides to grammar checkers to more how-to-write guidelines.

Avoiding Plagiarism

A simple rule to keep in mind is that anything that you copy from elsewhere should be quoted and cited, and anything that you paraphrase from someone else should be identified as coming from another source. Instructors don't want you to avoid citing, quoting, and paraphrasing. They do want you to be explicit about what is yours and what is drawn from someone else.

A very effective psychological test is used to detect plagiarism at a number of major universities, including the Armed Services Academies. The test is based on the psychological finding that a writer can easily reproduce his own writing but will have great difficulty reproducing someone else's writing. Students who are accused of plagiarism are asked to reproduce a section of the paper that they submitted as their own. If the student can closely reproduce the section, then the odds are extremely high that the student did indeed write the original paper. If the student cannot reproduce the original, the odds are equally high that the section was plagiarized.

TESTS AND OTHER ANXIETIES

Everyone who's ever taken an important test knows what it's like to feel "test anxiety," but some students find tests more intimidating than others do. In general, the best ways to cope with test anxiety are to (1) acquire effective study skills, (2) practice effective time management so that you are prepared for each test, and (3) know yourself as a learner and test taker so that you understand what helps and what hinders your performance in a testing situation.

Test preparation will vary depending on the kind of test that you will be taking, but everything you apply from your knowledge of study skills will contribute to your overall test preparation.

Test-Taking Skills for the Off-Campus Student

Here are some specific test-preparation tips adapted from study skills handouts used with adult students.

- You need to know from the beginning of the course how much material each test will cover—a chapter at a time, accumulative as you go along? Will the final test be comprehensive (over the entire book), everything covered in the book after a certain point, everything covered in the course (including lectures), or restricted to a certain topic?

- What percent of your total course grade will the test contribute? You need to weigh your study time accordingly.

- Have you been told what type of test will be given, or is the format unspecified? Some tests include a variety of types of questions (short answer, short essay, multiple-choice, fill-in-the-blanks, true/false).

- Start the test by reading the instructions carefully; do not jump into answering questions as fast as you can.

- A good rule is not to rush through the test; pace yourself so you don't run out of time, but use all the allotted time that you need. Check your test over carefully after finishing.

- In essay exams, it is usually a good idea to read all the questions before answering any. Then do some brief outline planning before answering. Write legibly because your instructor will be annoyed if she has to struggle to discern your words. Forcing the instructor to decipher words will distract from your meaning. Try to avoid any spelling or grammatical errors, and be sure to leave time for proofreading your answers before you turn in the exam. Always be sure when you reread your answers that you answered all of the questions asked.

- In multiple-choice questions, read all the choices before answering. As in true/false questions, be very cautious on all questions that use inclusive or exclusive words such as "always" or "never."

Mantra Meditation

Cardiologist Herbert Benson has done a series of research studies showing that the centuries-old practice of mantra meditation can be learned and applied effectively to lower tension, pulse rate, and blood pressure. Here's how to do mantra meditation. Start by picking a word or sound that you like, something that's easy to pronounce like "aahh," "ing," "oooh," or "ohm"—the meaning of the word is not important because all you want is a word or sound that you can easily repeat. Then set aside 10 minutes or so every day to sit quietly with your eyes closed and repeat the word over and over to yourself. Hear the word repeating inside your head. Of course, you will find that all sorts of thoughts and images intrude on your effort to do nothing except repeat your mantra. That's okay, simply start repeating the word or sound again as soon as you notice that you've been distracted. After practicing this meditation technique for a week, you should notice a definite quieting of your body and thoughts when you apply your mantra.

The way to use this technique in a test situation is to take 5 or 10 minutes before you go into the testing room and apply your mantra meditation. You should find that you are much less likely to get "speedy" and panicked in the test if you settle yourself down before the test begins.

Specific techniques can help you avoid test anxiety or cope with it when it happens. The old familiar advice to "count to 100," "take deep breaths," or "think of a beautiful scene that you like" is not bad advice to apply when you feel the jitters coming on. However, it is much more effective to actually practice a relaxation or meditation technique so that you make a habit of using it and knowing how it works before you get in to the test-taking situation. One such technique is "mantra meditation," as described in the box above.

Math Anxiety

A special form of anxiety that afflicts many students is math anxiety. For many students, difficulty with mathematical word problems stems from poor reading rather than poor skills in manipulating symbols.

The Learning Services Centre in Cambrian College employs six steps to help students to solve problems. Having the steps as a reference will help you develop good habits and keep you from freezing up in exams.

SIX STEPS IN SOLVING A PROBLEM

1. Read the problem carefully. Pay careful attention to wording. Underline key words and phrases. Don't mistake words that look similar but are not.

2. Read the problem again and see exactly what is given; see what values or numbers are provided.

3. See what principles apply. Every problem involves the application of certain principles or formulas, sometimes only one very simple one, maybe several. It is particularly important when studying courses that employ formulas, laws, rules, and so forth, not only to memorize them in their symbolic form but to understand the principles underlying their use and to be able to formulate them in your own words whenever possible.

4. The fourth step is fairly obvious—see how to apply the formula or principle. If the problem is fairly obvious, note what must be done first, then second, and so on. Occasionally, when there is a choice of procedures, use the one that appears simplest and most direct.

5. Carefully apply the principles and reach the solution. The word "carefully" is of maximum importance here. A large percentage of errors and lost marks are due to careless mistakes.

6. Finally, check your work. See whether the answer seems sensible, and check each computation.

Pay careful attention to the sixth step outlined above. A characteristic of "innumeracy" is that some people do not apply good sense to numbers and math problems in the way that they certainly would to other problems of everyday life. Instead, they simply follow formulas without really thinking about what they mean or understanding what would be a sensible range for an answer and what would be outside a sensible range.

There are a number of excellent books available to help students overcome math anxiety and achieve numeracy. If you are taking math or math-dependent courses and are worried about your ability to do well, consult one or more of these books and try to arrange to work with a math tutor. Tutoring in math and the sciences is a well-accepted practice, but students at a distance from a campus often are deprived of the benefits of tutoring. If possible, try to arrange for long-distance tutoring, which will show immediate and long-term benefits.

SOME FINAL TIPS FOR BECOMING A BETTER STUDENT

Listed below are several tips that will help you become a more effective learner—not just in distance learning classes but in any classroom or out-of-class learning project that you want to undertake.

- Take the time to read some how-to-study books available in libraries and bookstores. Check our Web site for some references. As with everything else, you need to select the techniques and ideas that work for you.

- Make a one-, two-, and three-year learning plan that lists, term by term, what you intend to study and how each course or project will contribute to your overall learning goals. Having a long-range plan will help you persist in those courses and assignments that are not inherently interesting but do relate to your goals. You may need to consult with your advisor to assemble the full plan, but sketch it out right away so that you have at least a general picture of when you will take which course and understand why each course is a part of your program.

- Use the ABC time management method at least one full term for your work, personal, and study life. Once you try for a term, you're likely to continue to use the method, at least whenever you are working under time pressures.

- Keep a study diary for a week. Recording how you feel doing assignments, reading textbooks, writing papers, solving problems, and taking tests will tell you a lot about how you approach a learning task and function as a learner.

- Find a study buddy. Research has demonstrated that it helps to study with someone else, especially in those courses that require extensive problem solving, such as mathematics, statistics, accounting, and science. If you are not meeting other students directly in class, arrange to communicate with your study partner via the telephone or email.

- Make an effort to meet with your instructors right away. You don't have to say anything profound or ask a difficult question, just begin to communicate. Once you start, it will be easier to ask for help when you really need it.

- Find something in the news that relates to what you are studying in each of your courses. It is important to take what you learn outside the textbooks and make connections to everyday life. Try talking to a friend or relative about what you are learning and explain how it connects to events in the news.

- Pretend that you are the instructor for the next chapter that you read. The most effective way to learn something is to "teach" it. Once you have prepared a short lecture and a short quiz that covers the chapter, you'll be approaching the subject from the active mind of an instructor, as a communicator and organizer, rather than from the passive mind of a passive student.

- Apply one of the learning theories that have been mentioned in this chapter to your own efforts as a learner. Check the Guide's Web site for more information.

- Reward yourself! Studying shouldn't be a dreaded grind. By treating yourself well as a student, you become a better student. By rewarding yourself with music, food, play, art, or whatever you choose, you can look forward to learning rather than dreading the time that you spend studying. Eventually, learning will become rewarding, and you will have changed your role or image as a student. In one view, this entire chapter has been about helping you make this shift. Learn for yourself, for pleasure, and to gain understanding versus learning for others, from fear, by trying to memorize.

Questions for Distance Learning Students to Ask Distance Learning Providers

Here are some straightforward questions to ask the institutional representatives where you are planning to take courses or pursue a degree. (See Chapter 2, "Choosing a Distance Education Provider," for additional and related questions.)

1 What tutoring services are available for distance learning students in the specific course that I'm planning to take? How do the tutoring services that are available for DL students compare with those that are provided for on-campus students?

2   Are instructors available by phone and/or email to answer questions that emerge from the lectures or the readings?

3   What is the student–teacher ratio for this course?

4   Is the instructor for this course a regular faculty member or a student assistant? Has the instructor taught the course before? Does the instructor teach the course on campus as well as off campus?

5   Can I view the syllabus for the course so that I will know about the requirements and grading before I take the course?

6   Is there information available about how students who have taken this course have evaluated the course and the instructor?

7   Will I have a single faculty advisor who will help me plan my degree program of courses and help me progress through the program?

Not every distance learning institution will have a full answer for every one of these questions, but the better ones will have satisfactory answers for at least some of the questions and will always be concerned about helping students do as well as they can in their courses.

SUMMARY: JUST A BEGINNING!

There is no conclusion to learning or to learning about learning. What you've acquired in this chapter is just a beginning that can be applied and extended as you use these study ideas and methods in different courses. You should try other approaches, devise your own, and reflect on your own growth as a learner. The person who has become a self-guided learner is capable of changing mere information into meaningful and useful ideas.

As educator Carl Rogers has stated, in quoting one of his own teachers: "Don't be a damn ammunition wagon, be a rifle." One of the greatest needs in our information age is for learners who can emerge from being information consumers to information evaluators and informed knowledge creators. At this level, learning becomes an art. Welcome to the never-ending art of learning!

CHAPTER 7

CAREER PLANNING

Building a Personal Life Plan

In this chapter you will

- ◆ analyze your own background, values, and needs, and complete several assessments that will help you explore different aspects of your personality

- ◆ characterize your own past experiences, jobs, and talents and match them with potential job opportunities and necessary skills

- ◆ determine if you are suited to a particular job or career, and design a career goal

- ◆ access data on the labor market, including changing employment outlooks, and complete a career informational interview

- ◆ look at each segment of the career planning process and evaluate that segment in developing your career plan

- ◆ acquire the necessary skills to secure your job—complete a thorough self-assessment, research potential employers, prepare cover letters and resumes, acquire interviewing techniques, and learn the various aspects of follow-up correspondence

INTRODUCTION

You are now in the last chapter of this book, and you are ready to get started on your course selection. It is difficult to select courses without knowing what your personal life plans are. Do you want to take a course to learn a new skill for work or leisure activities? Are you thinking of changing your career direction, or are you just beginning to consider what career you want to pursue? If you are ready to explore career options, this chapter will help you understand the importance of building a personal life plan and help you identify what you already have accomplished, consider what skills are transferable, and evaluate your prior learning and your strengths.

How will completing the career planning process help you? The work you choose will affect your entire life. Many human needs are influenced by a person's occupation. Needs such as self-esteem, achievement, autonomy, and power often are linked to an individual's occupation. Even basic physiological, security, and social needs may be affected by the work you pursue. In this incredibly complex world, your ability to deal with change and to achieve your personal goals will be linked to your career. Matching your personal lifestyle with your work lifestyle can provide a balance that enhances your life and can give you a high degree of life and work satisfaction. An imbalance can make you feel very dissatisfied and uncomfortable.

So now you are ready to begin this career planning process, but you are not quite sure what that means. Making plans for the future and deciding on a career are important life steps that have been researched and studied. Trained career counselors have identified five separate processes that they use to help people make these important decisions. This chapter will introduce you to these processes and help you prepare for your career journey. Internet resources and ways to access a career counselor will be identified. The chapter concludes with the job search process that will help you implement your career plan.

You should carefully complete the following processes from beginning to end. If you by-pass or lightly skim any of the concepts presented, you may miss an important element that would be helpful in planning your career. The learning objectives you will achieve after completing this chapter are listed in the process summary.

PROCESS I: SELF-EXPLORATION AND AWARENESS

Learning as much as possible about your preferred lifestyle, values, and needs, together with your background, personality, and skills, will help you evaluate career options and make an informed decision about a career. Ask yourself two questions. "What do I want out of life?" and "Where do I want to accomplish this?" Obviously, the second question is about geographic locations and types of employers, but the answer to the first question may not be so clear. The first question is asking you what you want to accomplish in your life. Do you want to be married or single, have children, live in the city or the country, own your own business, be involved in your community or church, be active in the arts or sports, work with people or work alone? All of these activities require you to make decisions. The decision that will have a tremendous influence on your life accomplishments is the decision you make about your life's work.

Background

Your background, regardless of your acceptance or rejection of the influences of your early life, will affect your values, your needs, and your goals. Take the time to review and study your background carefully. Many of the elements of our individual backgrounds unconsciously influence our decisions, regardless of the importance of the decision. Did you grow up in the city or the country? Were your parents divorced? Were there money issues, religious issues, and political issues that affected you and your family? Make a list of the issues or areas that you believe are influencing your decisions today by completing Exercise 7.1, "Background." These factors may be positive or negative. It is always helpful to be aware of events that are affecting your thoughts and actions.

Wants and Needs

Another area that influences our daily lives is making decisions about our wants and needs. Abraham Maslow devised a system that places needs and wants into a hierarchy. (See Figure 7.1, "Maslow's Hierarchy of Needs.") At the base of the pyramid are the basic survival or physiological needs such as food, clothing, rest, and safety. As these basic needs are met, a person can next concentrate on the

psychological levels of needs, which are social and esteem needs. At the top of the hierarchy are the self-actualization needs of achieving one's highest potential and realizing aesthetic or spiritual experiences.

Take the time to identify and rank your individual needs by completing Exercise 7.2, "Wants and Needs." By recognizing your individual needs and selecting a career that will help satisfy them, you can begin to meet your career and life expectations.

Values

Values are the foundation on which we make all of our daily decisions. For example, if your background has taught you that money is very important and you need to acquire as much as possible, this will influence you to enter a high-paying occupation over a low-

FIGURE 7.1

Maslow's Hierarchy of Needs.

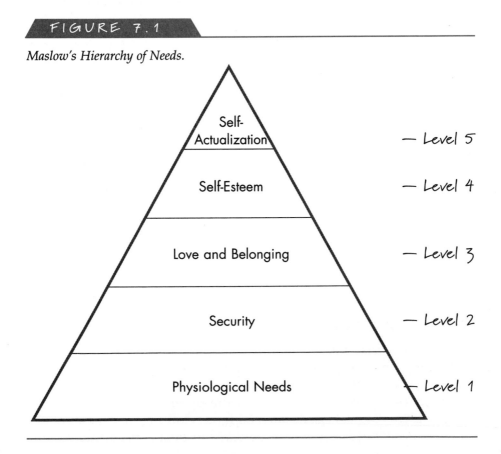

paying one. Money, family, work, religion, and personal agenda are five of the main value systems that will influence your decisions. Values can be tangible (material things, family) or intangible (love, social affiliation, adventure, excitement). Before you can use your values to help you make your decisions, you need to identify and prioritize them. Complete Exercise 7.3, "Values," which will help you to do this.

Personal Characteristics

Personal characteristics have a direct correlation to career fields and have been connected to job titles. The Myers/Briggs Type Indicator®[1] is a personality assessment that characterizes personality types using measures of extroversion versus introversion, sensing versus intuition, thinking versus feeling, and judging versus perceiving. See Figure 7.2 for a description of the 16 types. Most counselors and psychologists do not like to rely on just one instrument to measure personality traits. The FIRO-B (Fundamental Interpersonal Relations Orientation-Behavior™)[2] is a personality instrument that measures how you typically behave with other people and how you expect them to act toward you. As with the Myers/Briggs Type Indicator®, most of us are not only one type or the other. This instrument just helps you look at your most comfortable behavioral interactions. The Strong Interest Inventory™[3] is based on John L. Holland's career theory and characterizes people using six occupational interest types and work environments. The six occupational environment types are: realistic, investigative, artistic, social, enterprising, and conventional. See Figure 7.3 for a description of these types. As you can see, each of the instruments measures different aspects of personality. That is why it is so important in making a career decision to have as much information as you can about yourself. You can take these three inventories on the Internet and discuss the results with a counselor online or on the telephone. Use the Guide's Web site to access these inventories and career counselors to help with interpretation.

[1] Myers-Briggs Type Indicator and MBTI are registered trademarks of Consulting Psychologists Press, Inc.

[2] FIRO-B is a trademark of Consulting Psychologists Press, Inc.

[3] Strong Interest Inventory and SII are trademarks of Stanford University Press.

FIGURE 7.2

Myers/Briggs Type Indicator® Personality Characteristics.

ISTJ

Introverted Sensing with Thinking
Ability to organize tasks

Decisiveness
Follow-through
Can get things done
Maintain and preserve what works

ESTP

Extroverted Sensing with Thinking
Entrepreneurial approach

Crisis management
Ability to sell and promote
Adaptability
Willingness to take risks

ISFJ

Introverted Sensing with Feeling
Ability to get things organized

Preserve what works
Build consensus
People skills
Set up effective procedures

ESFP

Extroverted Sensing with Feeling
Adaptability

Enthusiasm and energy
Ability to motivate others
Negotiating and building consensus
Immediate problem-solving

INFJ

Introverted Intuition with Feeling
Imagination

Sense of purpose
Creativity
Ability to get things organized
Can develop human resources

ISTP

Introverted Thinking with Sensing
Analytical skills

Problem-solving ability
Technical knowledge and expertise
Adaptability
Willingness to take risks

ESTJ

Extroverted Thinking with Sensing
Ability to organize people and tasks

Analytical skills
Problem-solving at a functional level
Setting up and running effective
    procedures
Decisiveness

ISFP

Introverted Feeling with Sensing
Skilled at gentle persuasion

Craftsmanship
Adaptability
People skills
Can build consensus   *(continued)*

FIGURE 7.2

Continued.

ESFJ

Extroverted Feeling with Sensing
Ability to set up effective procedures

Decisiveness
Maintain and preserve what works
People skills
Skilled at building consensus

INFP

Introverted Feeling with Intuition
Sense of purpose

Creativity
People skills
Adaptability
Gentle persuasion

ENFP

Extroverted Intuition with Feeling
New ideas and possibilities

Enthusiasm and energy
People skills
Adaptability
Creativity

INTJ

Introverted Intuition with Thinking
Long-range vision

Analytical thinking
Problem-solving at a systems level
Conceptual design
Skill at planning

ENTP

Extroverted Intuition with Thinking
Creativity

Problem-solving at a systems level
Analytical skills
Technical expertise
Entrepreneurial approach

ENFJ

Extroverted Feeling with Intuition
Can get things organized

Ability to develop human resources
Skilled at building consensus
People skills
Energy and enthusiasm

INTP

Introverted Thinking with Intuition
Analytical skills

Problem-solving at a systems level
Technical knowledge and expertise
Adaptability
Conceptual design

ENTJ

Extroverted Thinking with Intuition
Can get things organized

Problem-solving at a systems level
Decisive
Analytical thinking
Long-range vision

FIGURE 7.3

The General Occupational Themes.

THEME	INTERESTS	WORK ACTIVITIES	POTENTIAL SKILLS	VALUES
Realistic (R)	Machines, tools, outdoors	Operating equipment, using tools, building, repairing	Mechanical ingenuity and dexterity, physical coordination	Tradition, practicality, common sense
Investigative (I)	Science, theories, ideas, data	Performing lab work, solving abstract problems, researching	Math, writing, analysis	Independence, curiosity, learning
Artistic (A)	Self-expression, art appreciation	Composing music, writing, creating visual art	Creativity, musical talent, artistic expression	Beauty, originality, independence, imagination
Social (S)	People, team-work, human welfare, community service	Teaching, explaining, helping	People skills, verbal ability, listening, showing understanding	Cooperation, generosity, service to others
Enterprising (E)	Business, politics, leadership, influence	Selling, managing, persuading	Verbal ability, ability to motivate and direct others	Risk taking, status, competition
Conventional (C)	Organization, data, finance	Setting up procedures, organizing, operating computers	Math, data analysis, record keeping, attention to detail	Accuracy, stability, efficiency

Exercise 7.1 Background.

Complete the following exercise to help you identify any issues you may have relating to your background/lifestyle. If you wish to complete this exercise for yourself on the Guide's Web site, go to the site, where an expanded form is provided.

1. I grew up in a _metropolitan_/rural/suburban area, which causes me to have the following feelings: *Example: I would like to live and work in a smaller, less populated city.*

   _____

   _____

2. Growing up, my relationship with my family (mother, father, siblings) was _good_, bad, indifferent. *Example: I had a very positive relationship with my family while growing up.*

   _____

   _____

3. I was the _oldest_, youngest, middle, only _girl_/boy in my family. My feelings about this are as follows: *Example: I enjoyed the responsibility given to me most of the time. However, I felt I was given too much at times, because I was the oldest.*

   _____

   _____

   _____

4. My parents' educational level attainment and income levels influenced my life in the following ways: *Example: My parents do not have a formal education, but I do want a B.S. degree in something.*

   _____

   _____

5. I would summarize my background and lifestyle as follows: (Include how you feel these issues influence your life now.) *Example: Middle class with a positive family environment. This has influenced me to seek a college degree.*

   _____

   _____

Exercise 7.2 Wants and Needs.

In the space provided, list the five most important wants that you must have in your life. Also list the five most important needs that you must have fulfilled. If you wish to complete this exercise for yourself on the Guide's Web site, go to the site, where an expanded form is provided.

Example

WANTS

1. New car
2. Good friend
3. Good job
4. College degree
5. _____

WANTS

1. _____
2. _____
3. _____
4. _____
5. _____

Example

NEEDS

1. Emotional security
2. Good relationships
3. Enough money to survive
4. _____
5. _____

NEEDS

1. _____
2. _____
3. _____
4. _____
5. _____

Now ask yourself:

- Are these realistic? *I hope so.*
- Are you willing to give up anything to have these? *I am willing to spend the time and money to obtain a college degree.*
- Will a career help you achieve these wants and needs? *I believe a career based on a college degree is a necessary requirement today.*

Exercise 7.3 Values.

Following are some of the values that most affect our lives. Evaluate them according to the importance you place on them. Circle the most appropriate response for you. (An example is provided. To complete this exercise on yourself in more depth, go to the Web site, where a form has been provided.)

FAMILY
Your mother, father, brother & sister, or your wife, husband, partner & children

Very Important		Important	Not Important	
5	(4)	3	2	1

MONEY
How you make money, spend it, and the amount you want to acquire

Very Important		Important	Not Important	
(5)	4	3	2	1

CAREER
The work you do daily to earn a living

Very Important		Important	Not Important	
(5)	4	3	2	1

FAITH
The involvement you have in your spiritual growth

Very Important		Important	Not Important	
5	4	3	2	(1)

PERSONAL AGENDA
Those activities in which you engage regardless of what else is occurring

Very Important		Important	Not Important	
5	4	(3)	2	1

LEISURE TIME
Able to pursue hobbies or other non-work activities

Very Important		Important	Not Important	
5	4	3	(2)	1

GEOGRAPHICAL LOCATION
Ability to live in any state you want or any location within a state

Very Important		Important	Not Important	
5	4	3	2	(1)

INDEPENDENCE
Ability to do what you want when and for how long you want

Very Important		Important	Not Important	
5	(4)	3	2	1

(continued)

Exercise 7.3 Continued.

RECOGNITION/PRESTIGE	Very Important		Important		Not Important
Be rewarded and recognized for what you do and who you are	⑤	4	3	2	1

SOCIAL ACCEPTANCE	Very Important		Important		Not Important
Involved with friends and membership in social clubs	5	4	3	②	1

VARIETY	Very Important		Important		Not Important
Able to work at different jobs or a variety of different aspects of a job	5	4	3	2	①

SUMMARIZE

Very Important Values	Important Values	Not Important Values
1. Money	1. Personal agenda	1. Faith
2. Career	2. Leisure time	2. Location
3. Family	3. Independence	3. Variety
4. Recognition	4.	4. Social Acceptance

DO YOU AGREE?

Let a close friend or family member look at your ranking and ask her what she has observed. Ask her to be honest and sincere in her response. You should be willing to accept her input graciously.

FOLLOW-UP

For the next two to three months, take an inventory of how much time, effort, and money you spend on each of these values. Then reevaluate and see if this ranking has changed.

PROCESS II: CAREER EXPLORATION AND AWARENESS

In Process I, you became aware of various aspects of your personality and how they might be impacting your actions, thoughts, and reactions to your environment. Now, link these with career possibilities. The second major process is identifying your past experiences and current skills and matching them with potential job opportunities and necessary skills. There are different kinds of skills, but they are usually divided into three areas.

- *Self-management* includes such skills as self-pacing, punctuality, and dependability. These skills are often linked to temperament and are acquired in early childhood.
- *Functional skills* are related to the ability to work with people, data, or things, and are transferable and linked to aptitudes.
- *Work content or specific content skills* are those skills needed for performing a job in a particular field or occupation. They are usually acquired in school, training, or on the job.

Please complete Exercise 7.4, "Data, People, Things," which will help you determine your skill level in these areas.

Past Experiences

A good place to start evaluating career possibilities is your past experiences. The direction for a successful new career may be found in the work experience you now have, the hobbies you enjoy, or your talents or past achievements. Please complete Exercise 7.5, "Achievements and Work Experiences," which is divided into two parts to help you analyze your past achievements and work experiences. The direction for a future successful career may be found in your list.

Dictionary of Occupational Titles

Work can be organized in a variety of ways. Due to technological, economic, and sociological influences, most jobs are performed differently from any other job. However, every job can also be related to a number of similar jobs. These similarities have been used to organize the **Dictionary of Occupational Titles** (DOT). In the DOT, all jobs are listed by occupational title with a nine-digit code. The middle three digits of the code will provide an evaluation of the skill level needed for data, people, and things. A description of task elements is listed, as well as other related titles. The jobs are categorized by occupational divisions, such as clerical and sales, machine trades, and professional, technical, and managerial occupations. Analyze the example in Figure 7.4 so that you understand all of the components.

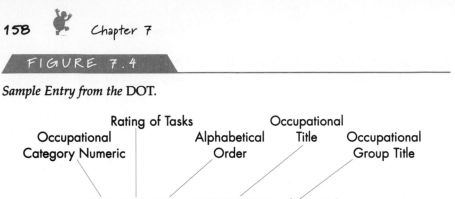

FIGURE 7.4

Sample Entry from the DOT.

Rating of Tasks   Occupational
Occupational   Alphabetical   Title   Occupational
Category Numeric   Order   Group Title

001.061-010 ARCHITECT (profess. & kin.)

Researches, plans, designs, and administers building projects for clients, applying knowledge of design, construction procedures, zoning and building codes, and building materials. Consults with client to determine functional and spatial requirements of new structure or renovation, and prepares information regarding design, specifications, materials, color, equipment, estimated costs, and construction time. Plans layout of project and integrates engineering elements into unified design for client review and approval. Prepares scale drawings and contract documents for building contractors. Represents client in obtaining bids and awarding construction contracts. Administers construction contracts and conducts periodic on-site observation of work during construction to monitor compliance with plans. May prepare operating and maintenance manuals, studies, and reports. May use computer-assisted design software and equipment to prepare project designs and plans. May direct activities of workers engaged in preparing drawings and specification documents.

Occupational Outlook Handbook

Another valuable resource is the **Occupational Outlook Handbook (OOH),** which provides information about careers in eight different categories:

1. Nature of the work
2. Working conditions
3. Employment opportunities
4. Training, other qualifications, and advancement
5. Job outlook
6. Earnings
7. Related occupations
8. Sources of additional information

Career Clusters

Groups of similar occupations are called career clusters because they are functionally related. Career clusters usually require the same or related skills, education, and experience. For example, the business occupational cluster (see Figure 7.5, "Occupational Families/Clusters for Business") is divided into separate, yet related fields of accounting, management, economics, marketing, finance, and personnel. It is a good idea to broaden your initial career search to include fields related to your initial interests. Maybe a related field would be of greater interest or give you greater satisfaction than your first idea. You can use the **Occupational Outlook Handbook** to review related occupations.

 This document can also be accessed on the Internet using the directions described on the Guide's Web site. **Please** complete Exercise 7.6, "Employment Projections."

FIGURE 7.5

Occupational Families/Clusters for Business.

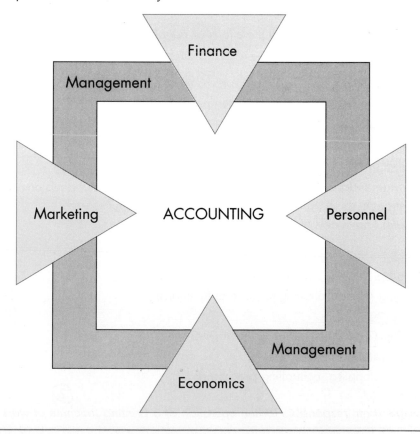

Exercise 7.4 Skills, Data, People, Things.

Directions: After identifying your competency level in the skills listed below, write two or three examples of activities with which you have been involved that demonstrate you have that skill.

Indicate skill level using this scale: 1, weak; 2, average; 3, strong. To complete this exercise relating to yourself, go to the Web site for this handbook. An expanded form is provided.

DATA   Example:

Synthesizing
(Integrating & analyzing)
How strong?   1   ②   3
Example: I have compared information, but never really analyzed data.

Coordinating
(Determine time, place, sequence)
How strong?   1   ②   3
Example: I have coordinated the efforts of people at my work.

PEOPLE

Mentoring
(Dealing with total personality to advise or counsel)
How strong?   ①   2   3
Example: I have never done anything like this.

Negotiation
(Exchanging ideas & information to formulate policy or make decisions)
How strong?   ①   2   3
Example: I have never done any negotiating.

THINGS

Setting Up
(Adjusting or programming to perform functions)
How strong?   1   2   ③
Example: Have done basic computer programming.

Operation-Controlling-Driving
(Starting, stopping, controlling processes)
How strong?   1   ②   3
Example: I am responsible for the operation of a printing machine at work.

Exercise 7.5a Achievements.

Directions: In the space provided, list all achievements that you have experienced in your life. Indicate what satisfaction you gained from each. To complete this exercise on yourself, go to the Web site, where an expanded form is provided.

Achievement	What Satisfaction Did This Achievement Give Me?
1. Example: I play the piano.	It calms me down and relaxes me when I am stressed. Playing helps me think through my problems.
2.	
3.	
4.	
5.	
6.	
7.	

Exercise 7.5b Work Experience.

Directions: In the space provided, list all of the work experience you have ever had, indicating assignments, the positive and negative aspects, and why you enjoyed certain areas of the work. To complete this exercise on yourself, go to the Web site, where an expanded form is provided.

Title of Work Experience	Example: Carpenter's helper	
Assignments/ Responsibilities	Measuring and cutting lumber	
Most Positive Aspect	I got to work with my hands	
Why Did I Enjoy Those Areas of the Work?	Satisfaction in seeing what I helped build	
Negative Aspects	I got dirty	

Exercise 7.6a Employment Projections.

The Bureau of Labor Statistics Office of Employment Projects has the latest employment outlook information. To learn more, access their Web site at

http://stats.bls.gov/emphome.htm

At this Web site, you will be able to learn about employment projects, the fastest growing jobs, the fastest growing industries, and occupational projections. To get information on the specific occupations in which you have an interest, follow these instructions:

1. Click on *Occupational Outlook Handbook.*
2. Select one of the search areas.

Exercise 7.6b The Occupational Information Network (O*Net) (Formerly DOT and OOH).

The O*Net is an easy-to-use database that runs on a Windows-based personal computer. It contains comprehensive information on job requirements and work competencies. O*Net replaces the *Dictionary of Occupational Titles* and offers a more dynamic framework for exploring the world of work. General areas of information are: "Experience Requirements," "Occupational Requirements," "Occupation Specifics," "Occupation Characteristics," "Work Characteristics," and "Worker Requirements."

For more information on O*Net and to acquire information on your career goals, visit O*Net at:

O*Net@doleta.gov

http://www.doleta.gov/programs/onet/

PROCESS III: CAREER PLANNING AND GOAL SETTING

You have accumulated a significant amount of information about yourself and researched several career positions. Now, it is time to make some initial decisions. First, it is helpful to examine the flow involved in making a decision and to clarify how decisions are made. A good first step is to examine the difference between a job and a career. Generally, a job is viewed as something that can provide for the basic needs of life: food, clothing, shelter, and transportation. A career has a greater purpose and meaning and usually gives far more personal satisfaction than a job.

Review the list of your personal needs, which includes your background/lifestyle concerns, your values, and your wants and/or needs. Next, compare it to the outline on the differences in Figure 7.6, "Career/Job—A Comparison." This will help you focus on a career path rather than on one specific job.

Sectors

Another important part of your decision will be to consider the employment sector in which you want to work. Three sectors usually are considered. The public sector is working for local, state, or federal government. The private sector is composed of large and small corporations and companies. The self-employed sector is working for

yourself, either in a business or providing some type of service. Working in each sector has both advantages and disadvantages. Review the chart in Figure 7.7, "Employment Sector." Satisfaction in your career, in part, is determined by your satisfaction with the primary mission of the organization in which you are employed.

Career Goals

You should now try to list three different career goals. For example, you may be skilled at mathematics, like detail, and enjoy working with things. Initially, three possible goals are: to be a CPA, a mathematics teacher, or an electrical engineer. These are tentative goals at this point based on your initial research. The next process is to gather information on your three career goals to give you the insight to proceed with your career decision.

INITIAL CAREER GOALS (EXAMPLE)

1. CPA
2. Mathematics teacher
3. Electrical engineer

The next section will help you in gathering career information.

FIGURE 7.6

Career/Job—A Comparison.

Career	Job
■ Specific mission/goal	■ Means to an end
■ Deliberate steps with a plan	■ Routine, not steps
■ High expectations for personal growth	■ Little or low personal growth/ satisfaction/feeling of accomplishment
■ Academic goals are met through career	■ On-the-job training, low dedication
■ Personal goals are met through career	■ Personal goals and work goals not compatible
■ Professionalism and high degree of personal integrity	■ Employer's goals and personal goals normally not similar
	■ Temporary employment

FIGURE 7.7

Employment Sectors.

	Public Sector	Private Industry	Self-Employed
Advancement	Judged by knowledge and skill	Judged by performance and political skill	Judged by personal abilities, skill, and performance
Money (Rewards)	Nonmonetary, low pay for degree of responsibilities	Good, based more on personal performance	Profits or losses go to owner; high-risk
Benefits/ Retirement Compensation	Good	Changing; fewer positions have full benefits, employee contribution has increased	Costs go to owner, many benefits may not be available
Control	Political	More control within guidelines	Total control
Time Commitment	Normal 40-hour week	Whatever it takes, within limits	24 hours a day, 7 days a week
Decision Making	Normal chain of command	Dictated by amount and degree of authority	Decisions good and bad
Security	Good	Judged by personal performance	High-risk, highly self-motivated, disciplined
Purpose	Service	Profit	Profit/Service

PROCESS IV: CAREER DATA INFORMATION GATHERING

Before you can decide on your career goal, you need to research the required education and potential employers for each of the three careers you identified in Process III. Maybe it is not possible for you to spend the required years attending college. Maybe you can't stand to work in an office eight hours a day. Before you spend your time and money pursuing a major field of study, you need to have firsthand knowledge of working conditions, atmosphere, challenges, type of duties, educational requirements, licenses, salary and promotion expectations, job and career expectations, skills, and scope of career/employer options. You can obtain this information in two ways: (1) identifying potential employers on the Internet through their Web sites; and (2) conducting fact-finding interviews in person with individuals who currently work in your identified career area.

Identifying Potential Employers

You can begin this process by accessing general employment databases on the Internet. Examples of these databases are listed in Figure 7.8, found on the following pages. The most up-to-date list

can be found on the Guide's Web site. Visit several of these databases and identify potential employers in your three career areas. Use this information to access employers' Web sites to obtain more specific information.

Fact-Finding Interview

After you have researched the careers and employers on the Internet, you should conduct a fact-finding interview. The employer's Web site will usually list an address, telephone number, business hours, and contact person. You may also want to go to the career center or placement office located at the university or college near you. They will usually have personal knowledge of local employers to contact for an interview. Local chambers of commerce often maintain directories of employers. You may conduct the interview over the telephone, but a personal visit to the actual work environment is very helpful.

Several interviewing hints are listed below. Incorporating these suggestions will help you acquire pertinent information you need to make an informed decision.

1. Be familiar with the research you have conducted on the employer.
2. Make an appointment by telephone or email.

2

3. Know the questions you want to ask the employer.
4. Ask permission to tape the interview. This will ensure that you retain any important information.
5. Do not be late for your appointment.
6. Dress professionally; wear appropriate business attire.
7. Do not smoke or chew gum.
8. Document your perceptions and findings after your interview.
9. Send a thank-you letter after the interview.

Use the form in Exercise 7.7, "Fact-Finding Interview" (page 169), as a guide to structure your questions.

Although conducting one interview with a person who currently works in your interest area is good, it is much better if you can interview three or four people in the same career field. Multiple interviews give you better insight into the preparation required for the field and what you will actually encounter as an employee. After conducting your interviews, you need to reflect on the information you have obtained and try to imagine yourself in that career field. Does the career fit you? Does it complement your lifestyle, values, immediate family expectations, salary needs, personal goals, and retirement expectations? Could you do it day after day? Are you willing to complete the required course work and training?

FIGURE 7.8

Sample Databases. (For more listings, go to the Guide's Web site.)

GENERAL EMPLOYMENT DATABASES

America's Employers—comprehensive job search site for professionals, managers, and executives. Includes links to a number of other job sites, plus a resume bank and other job hunting advice and information:
http://www.americasemployers.com

Career Mosaic—lists a number of high-tech employers. Career Mosaic also has a searchable index of jobs posted to over 20 job-related newsgroups:
http://www.service.com/cm/cml.html

(continued)

FIGURE 7.8

Continued.

CareerWEB—global recruitment service, listing jobs worldwide that job seekers may access for free. Employers and recruitment companies may place their job listings worldwide:
http://www.cweb.com

The Monster Board—an interactive database for listing and locating job opportunities with America's hottest companies:
http://www.monster.com

NEWSPAPER ADS ON THE INTERNET

AdSearch—a collection of classified ads from a number of newspapers across the country. These ads are placed by Miller Advertising Agency, Inc., one of the largest recruitment ad agencies in the nation. Has a Job Search section. Job openings stay on AdSearch for at least two weeks:
http://www.adsearch.com

Employment Online—contains the classifieds of five newspapers: *The News & Observer,* Raleigh, NC; *The News Tribune,* Tacoma, WA; *The Sacramento Bee,* Sacramento, CA; *The Modesto Bee,* Modesto, CA; and the *Anchorage Daily News,* Anchorage, AK:
http://www.nando.net/classads/employment/careers.html

National Ad Search—newspaper version of the National Ad Search provides the most complete coverage of job opportunities in the nation:
http://www.nationaladsearch.com

USA Today—a searchable database of all national, regional, and local employment ads from the *USA Today* newspaper. Part of the Best Jobs In the *USA Today* site:
http://bestjobsusa.com

SAMPLE COMPANIES ON THE INTERNET

American Stores Company:
http://www.oscodrug.com

Boeing Company:
http://www.boeing.com

Federal Bureau of Investigation:
http://www.odci.gov/usic/fbi.html

Firestone:
http://www.firestone.co

Exercise 7.7 Fact-Finding Interview.

To acquire depth and breadth in your interview, use the following questions as a guide. Add any questions that are important to you. To complete this exercise, go to our Web site, where an expanded format is provided.

1. Name and title of individual
2. Number of years at present organization
3. Number of years in the field
4. Current duties/responsibilities
5. What are the educational requirements of your position?
   Number of years of training/college   *Certification/licenses*
   Major field of study   *Related experience requirement*
6. What were your reasons for entering the field?
   (circumstances/decisions/by chance)
7. Describe the career potential and mobility options in this field.
8. What related positions are available?
9. What skills or competencies are required?
   People interaction   *Physical condition*
   Social involvement   *Leadership & initiative*
   Academic ability   *Quantitative computation*
   Computer competency
10. What is the work atmosphere?
    Outside   *Team/Group*
    Indoors   *Autonomy*
    Office
11. What are the rewards?
    Starting salary
    Mid-range salary
    Seasoned employee (after 10–15 years)
    Benefits
12. What are the challenges and opportunities in your field?
    Stress level   *Creativity*
    Frustrations   *Initiation*
    Hassles   *Problem solving*
13. What is your recommendation on the steps necessary to enter the field?
14. What are the three strongest aspects/advantages of your field?
15. What are the three most negative aspects of your field?
16. What personality type or temperament type excels in this career field?
17. Is there anyone else you would suggest I contact for more information?

PROCESS V: CAREER REVIEW AND ADJUSTMENT

During your work life, you may change careers two, three, or maybe four times before you retire. Each time you should repeat the same processes you have learned in this chapter. A review of where you are in your life and career is a healthy and beneficial experience. After you conduct a review, you may decide to make adjustments, or a career change or transition. Transitions are easi-er if you have the necessary information and tools to make these critical decisions. Go to the Web site and use the form in Exercise 7.8, "Summary of Your Findings," to help you summarize and prioritize your previous work.

After completing this summary, you should be able to list the two occupations or careers that seem appropriate for you. If you are still undecided, you may want to review the exercises again, interview more people in your interest area, or contact a career counselor at a college or university near you.

Career Plan

You now should be ready to design a career plan. You can use the form in Exercise 7.9, "Educational/Employability Plan," to help you meet your career goal. Most career goals will require three to six major action steps to complete. For example, if your goal is to be an electrician, you may be required to take one year of basic electronics classes and complete three or four years of apprenticeship. Becoming a physician has many more steps: (1) complete four years of college, (2) complete four years of medical school, (3) complete a one- to two-year internship, (4) complete one to two years of residency, (5) establish a practice. As you can see, it is very important for you to know the major action steps involved in your career.

Now that you have designed your plan, you need to break your long-range goals into short-range goals and develop a timetable identifying when you expect to reach each short-range goal. Use the form in Exercise 7.10, "Peterson's Guide," to help you identify college and program curricula that will meet your long-term educational goal.

Exercise 7.9 Educational/Employability Plan.

To complete this exercise for yourself, go to our Web site.

The occupation or career I plan to pursue is: Accounting

I. The major educational steps, or requirements, involved are:

(Example)

1. Be accepted to College of Business Accounting program
2. Earn B.S. degree – Accountancy
3. _____
4. _____
5. _____

II. Activities involved in each step/requirement:

(Example)

Step #1

Acceptance to College of Business Accountancy program

Activities

1. Complete generals
2. Complete core requirements for College of Business
3. _____
4. _____

Step #2

Earn B.S. degree in Accountancy Activities

Activities

1. Complete major requirements
2. Complete minor requirements
3. Complete all major field courses
4. Meet all upper division requirements
   (minimum 60 credit hours)

Exercise 7.10 Peterson's Guide.

You have now identified at least one or more occupations that interest you. Gaining knowledge about the necessary college or university training requirements is your next step.

In addition to learning about the required academic curriculum and/or training for your desired occupations, you need to identify the best college/university to attend. One of the best sources for school information, which also will give you the required curriculum, is the *Peterson's Guides*. Peterson's is known as the country's largest education information and communication company. They provide information on private schools, colleges and universities, graduate and professional schools, international study, adult learning, and career guidance. You can visit Peterson's Education Center on the Internet at **http://www.peterson.com**

Following is a list of the individual volumes/directories available on the Web or in hard copy:

Two-Year Colleges
Four-Year Colleges
Study Abroad
Professional Program
  Overview

Graduate Programs in:
  Biological Sciences
  Humanities, Arts, Social Sciences
  Business, Education, Health Information
    Studies, Law, and *Social Work*
  Physical Sciences, Mathematics, and
    Agricultural Science,
  Engineering and Applied Sciences

After reviewing the programs and schools in the *Peterson's Guides,* you may want to look up, on the Internet, the schools in your local community or state and see what programs are available. As you review the availability of schools and academic programs, keep in mind the following questions:

1. Which school is the best to attend for my field of interest?

2. How many years of school and/or degrees must I complete?

3. Will I be required to leave my home state? Am I willing to do that?

4. Are my basic skills, reading, math, writing, and computer literacy strong, or will I have to be involved in remedial or prerequisite courses?

5. What are the costs involved in attending the school of my choice? Can I afford it?

6. Do I have the level of personal commitment to finish the required academic program?

PROCESS VI: JOB SEARCH

As you near completion of your career plan, you will need to begin the job search process. This portion of the chapter will provide only a summary of the process you need to use to acquire the skills to find your job. Return to this section when you are ready to actually begin job searching. Although this process is divided into steps, you need to be doing several of the activities concurrently.

Research Employer

Researching potential employers is the first activity. Knowing about a company or agency will enhance your answers to the interviewer's questions. You have had experience researching companies using their Web sites and conducting your informational interviews. This research is even more important when you are going to interview for a job.

Self-Assess

While you are doing your research on companies and agencies, don't forget to assess yourself. Review your skills and abilities, related and nonrelated work experience, and training. Employers are looking for employees who are skilled and meet their needs. Knowledge in your field and related work experience, such as completing an internship or a cooperative work experience, are important to employers. Your communication and social skills are also very important. Employers also seek employees who are mobile and willing to move to a different location.

Prepare Resume

After you have done your self-assessment, you are ready to prepare your resume. A well-prepared resume can be a valuable tool in helping you find a position. You should design or tailor your resume to reflect the requirements of each position for which you apply. There are three basic types of resumes used in business, industry, and the private sector. The *reverse chronological* resume moves the reader from the present back through time to show how you have arrived at your present position. This type of resume usually includes a professional

objective, education, educational highlights, work experience, special skills and abilities, background and interests,
and references. See Figure 7.10, "Reverse Chronological
Resume," which is on our Web site.

The *functional* resume is designed to focus on your specific skills
and abilities. These skills are usually transferable from one work environment to another. This type of resume is particularly helpful for
people with significant work experience of ten, fifteen, or twenty years,
and for people with little work experience but who have done significant volunteer or other unpaid work, such as Scouting, community, or
church work. This format is also helpful for people making a career
change or transition, such as retiring from the military. New graduates
who want to work in a field not directly related to their major, as well
as liberal arts graduates, find this resume very helpful. See
Figure 7.11, "Functional Resume," located on the Web site.

A resume that is becoming more popular is the *combination* (Functional/Chronological) resume. This format groups
related employment experiences based on the identified needs of the
employer. See Figure 7.12, "Sample Combination Resume," on the
Web site.

Increasingly, companies are using various electronic formats to
process resumes. Scanning is popular with large companies, and this
trend is spreading to small companies. Computers read resumes differently than people do. Consider these important tips to generate a
computer-friendly resume:

- **Focus on nouns, not verbs.** Job computers rarely search for words
  like *inspired, built, represented,* or *verified.* Yes, your resume should
  include action verbs for sentence flow and human eyes, but the
  keywords for an accountant might be *B. S. Accounting, accounts
  payable, IRS Amendments,* and *CPA.* If your resume doesn't contain
  these keywords, the computer won't select your resume.

- **Keep it simple.** Don't create a "top this" display of fonts and
  design. Computers adore simplicity. Follow these guidelines:

  Use popular, nondecorative typefaces. Use a font size of
  10–14 points. Use light-colored standard size paper ($8\,1/_2$" x 11"
  in the U. S.), printed on one side only. Avoid italics, script,
  underlined text, graphics, and shading. It's okay to use capital-
  ized and bold-faced words. Avoid staples and folds. Avoid
  horizontal and vertical lines. Your name should be the first item
  on each page.

Prepare Cover Letter

Keep in mind that your resume does not stand by itself. You will need to introduce yourself and convince the reader that she should look at your resume carefully. The same rules apply to cover letters and resumes. Tailor your letter to the position. Do not use form letters that you send to multiple firms. Make it personal and specific for each company or agency. If you are granted an interview, you will want to send a thank-you letter to the individual who interviewed you. Examples of these two letters are found in Figures 7.12 and 7.13, located on the Web site.

Interviewing Process

The interview process actually begins when you get up in the morning. Get a good night's sleep, eat breakfast, shower, and dress in a professional manner. Plan to arrive early. This extra time will leave room for unforeseen events such as flat tires, arriving at the wrong office, and so forth. These extra minutes will give you an opportunity to check your appearance one last time, get acquainted with the environment, and prepare mentally for the actual interview. It is helpful to tape yourself in a mock interview, or rehearse several times with a friend, before the actual day of the interview.

Remember that interviews involve two-way communication between you and the employer. They are much more than a series of questions for you to answer. The actual interview is usually divided into five major components. You should keep in mind that you and the employer both have objectives. If you understand both your objectives and the interviewer's objectives, you will be more comfortable and will be able to present yourself in a more natural way.

The Interview: Component I—Introduction. This establishes a common ground for communication and usually lasts about 3–5 minutes.

The employer's objectives are to: (1) obtain an initial, overall impression of you; (2) set a communication base relative to tone of voice, thought patterns, and idea expression.

Your objectives are to: (1) give a positive first impression; (2) identify those skills and abilities the employer is seeking that will help you custom fit your answers; (3) establish a clear communication base to ensure you will have a thorough understanding of the communication exchange during the rest of the interview.

The next three phases are the main body of the interview. The employer will be seeking information regarding your work history, work experience, training, and skills, and will be evaluating your communication and interpersonal skills.

The Interview: Component II—Work History and Experience. The employer will be trying to understand the type and competency level of your past work experiences.

The employer's objectives are to: (1) establish your competency level and experience relative to the position; (2) determine how fast you will learn and progress in the company's environment; (3) measure your ability to handle pressure and be a team player; (4) assess your past performance against your stated accomplishments; (5) establish if your past work performance is an accurate measure of your future performance.

Your objectives are to: (1) show the employer that you have the skills and abilities he or she is seeking; (2) emphasize your past performance and accomplishments that are related to the company's needs; (3) evaluate the position and determine if it will fit into your long-range career goals; (4) demonstrate strong interest in the position and company by asking sincere and thoughtful questions; (5) demonstrate your competency level and potential future value to the employer's organization.

The Interview: Component III—Education, Training, and Abilities. As you complete your classes and graduate, your college work will be a very positive factor in your favor.

The employer's objectives are to: (1) assess and compare your educational preparation against the needs of the organization; (2) determine your ability to apply the theoretical concepts in the actual work environment; (3) assess your attitude toward learning to predict your progress in the company.

Your objectives are to: (1) relate your educational preparation directly to the employer's needs as you understand the position, duties, and responsibilities; (2) demonstrate your ability to apply theoretical concepts gained from projects, assignments, or related experience to the work environment; (3) emphasize your continued desire to learn and progress in the organization through additional study, company-sponsored training, and acceptance of challenges.

The Interview: Component IV—Communication and Interpersonal Skills.

Throughout the interview, the employer will observe your communication and interpersonal skills.

The employer's objectives are to: (1) identify your level of self-esteem and maturity; (2) evaluate your interpersonal skills and assess your ability to work with current employees; (3) evaluate your ability to communicate ideas to another person; (4) determine if your interpersonal style may cause conflict or problems in a team effort.

Your objectives are to: (1) demonstrate self-confidence and emotional maturity; (2) demonstrate your ability to get along with others and relate to all people; (3) demonstrate your communication skills and abilities; (4) de-emphasize any negative aspects of your interpersonal style.

The Interview: Component V—Summary.

The employer's objectives are to: (1) assess your interest in the position; (2) answer any questions you may have regarding the duties or responsibilities of the position; (3) ensure the employer has all the information necessary to make a decision.

Your objectives are to: (1) identify the level of interest the employer has in you; (2) ensure the employer understands your skills and that you will be able to perform the responsibilities of the desired position; (3) determine the appropriate follow-up procedures after the interview.

The interviewer should not ask you questions relating to:

Age	Military discharge
Date of birth	Home ownership status
Number of children	Memberships in organizations
Marital status	Maiden name
Race	Garnishment history

Faith   Significant other status

Arrest record   People who live with you

These are illegal questions because they ask about personal information unrelated to the position qualifications.

When you are trying to decide which job and employer to select, you must take into consideration your personal values and the impact your decision will have on those values. If you have a strong family value system that would require you to be home every night, a career decision that would require you to travel out of town 15 to 20 nights per month may be damaging to that value. You also have to evaluate each offer based on whether or not the position will help you reach your ultimate career goals rather than how much money you are going to make or the geographic location of the job.

For additional information about resumes, interviewing, and other job-seeking skills, visit the Career Center Internet Web site of universities and colleges. Those centers that have online assistance for employment skills are listed on the Guide's Web site.

Now that you have completed this chapter on career planning and decision making, you may want to take a career development class for credit and obtain additional information on the processes you have reviewed. Career development classes online are listed on our Web site.

SUMMARY: A FINAL THOUGHT

In this concluding chapter, we have emphasized the importance of life planning, whether related to work or fun, in your learning. Exploring career options from the very beginning of your educational experience, and at all points along the way, is the way to ensure you end up where you want to be—in terms of your education, your lifestyle, and your career.

As we said at the beginning of the chapter, matching your personal lifestyle with your work lifestyle can provide a balance that enhances your life and provides you with a high degree of life and work satisfaction. We should strive for nothing less.

Final Word

When we hear the term *pioneer,* we may think of the great events of history, such as Columbus's voyages to the New World or the first space flight to the moon. On a smaller scale, though, you are among those pioneers. You have entered the brave new world of "virtual higher education."

This book has been your guide on this new journey. Rather than having a human navigator to help you avoid the rocks and shoals of the trip, you have had a "virtual team" of guides who have given you a dynamic map of this new educational world.

Because distance learning is new and dynamic, it is also very exciting. Where our traditional campus and classroom structures have been in place for hundreds of years, distance learning is emerging rapidly as a new educational culture. This culture departs dramatically from the classroom-based educational structure that we have all experienced. And, of greatest importance, rather than the professor being at the center of this new instructional process, you, the learner, are now at the center.

All of this discussion about distance learning and the ways in which it differs from traditional learning should not lead you to conclude that classrooms and professors are being replaced. Quite the opposite is true. Distance learning is changing the scope and scale of education. By using electronic technologies, it is expanding the size of the classroom (by sending education beyond the classroom walls) and it is extending the reach of professors to learners (wherever they are located) by providing a variety of distance learning options.

This Guide has provided you with a detailed introduction to this new world of distance learning and a variety of navigational tools to help you on your educational journey. Chapter 1 introduced you to distance learning and Chapter 2 told you who provides it and how to choose a provider. Chapters 3 and 4 provided detailed information about the two tools most critical to your success—the computer and the virtual library. Chapters 5 and 6 provided information and advice about how to be a successful student and how to maintain balance in your life as you are learning. And, finally, Chapter 7 prepared you to use your learning in and for the world of work.

Of most importance, the Guide has emphasized that your educational journey never ends. Your new skills for learning in an electronic and virtual world will be used repeatedly as you return to education—to expand your horizons, to remain current in your career, or as you develop new skills to help you change jobs or careers a number of times in your working life.

And so we have come full circle. The Preface to this Guide began by discussing Aesop's 2,500-year-old fable about the tortoise and the hare. For the tortoise, the race was a pioneering effort. She did not know what the future held. But, in winning the race, she showed that pioneering persistence pays off—that "slow and steady wins the race."

It is the same in education. The slow and steady mastery of the information and advice in this Guide is one of the keys to success in distance learning. As you access learning in future years, return and visit us. You may have missed some things of interest on your first trip. We look forward to being your navigator in the future in the ever-changing world of distance learning!

Contributing Authors

David Bilyeu (Chapter 4) is College Librarian at Central Oregon Community College and University Center in Bend, Oregon. He has served on many state library committees and has worked on distance education issues throughout Oregon. David has consulted with the Western Interstate Commission for Higher Education in formulating a plan for library services for the Western Governors University. He has held positions at Caltech in Pasadena, Cabrillo College in Santa Cruz, and Westmont College in Santa Barbara, California. He has a B. A. in philosophy from the University of California, Santa Cruz, and a master's degree in library and information science from Syracuse University.

Susan M. Campbell (Chapter 5) is Director of Advising Services at the University of Southern Maine. She received her B. S. in speech and theater from Ball State University, her M. S. in adult education from the University of Southern Maine, and her Ed. D. from the University of Massachusetts at Amherst. Susan has over 20 years of experience in academic and student affairs administration and has held administrative positions in financial aid, admissions, summer session, and off-campus education. She teaches undergraduate courses in student leadership and graduate courses in both organizational management and student affairs. Her research and practice interests include student development, adult learning, enrollment management, academic advising, and career planning.

George P. Connick (Chapter 2) is the founder and President Emeritus of the Education Network of Maine, the statewide distance learning network of the University of Maine system. During his 31-year association with the University of Maine system, he held various faculty and administrative positions, including nine years as the president of the University of Maine at Augusta (1985–94) and three years as president of the Education Network of Maine (1994–97). He has delivered more than 300 presentations on the uses of technology and telecommunications for distance learning, and he is the author of numerous articles and reports on a variety of educational topics. George is currently the President of Distance Education Publications, Inc., a publishing company he founded in 1990. He also serves as a consultant to numerous

higher education institutions in the United States and Canada on issues related to distance education. He earned his B. A. from Stanford University, an M. A. from San Jose State University, and a Ph. D. in history from the University of Colorado at Boulder.

Steven H. Eichmeier (Chapter 7) is the Director of Career Services (career planning, cooperative education, and internship and employment) at Weber State University (WSU) in Ogden, Utah. Steve holds a doctorate in curriculum design and instructional methods from Brigham Young University. His B. S. and M. S. degrees in marketing are from Utah State University. Steve is involved in the annual national employment of more than 3,000 WSU students. He teaches weekly seminars on career planning, job-seeking skills, and resources. In addition to 29 years of teaching and counseling experience at Weber State, he has served as a consultant to several U. S. training institutes on employment and career planning, and he has written three books.

Joseph Hart (Chapter 6) is the Director of Distance Learning at Eastern Oregon University. He received his B. A. degree from Lewis and Clark College in psychology, his M. S. from the University of Wisconsin in clinical psychology, and his Ph. D. from Stanford University in experimental psychology. He has taught and served as an academic administrator on the faculties of the University of California, Irvine; the University of Southern California; the University of Redlands, Whitehead Center; and the California State Polytechnic University in Pomona. He received an outstanding faculty teaching award at the University of Redlands for his work with adult students. Joe has written a variety of monographs, chapters, and articles on a range of subjects, which have appeared in various scientific journals. He has been involved with computer-mediated instruction since the early 1970s. His current work is focused on the development of multimedia-enhanced Web-based courses.

Fred Hurst (Chapter 3) is the founding Executive Director of the Florida Public Postsecondary Distance Learning Institute (since January 1997). The Institute was created by the State University and Community College systems of Florida and is responsible for developing distance learning policies and procedures that ensure cooperation and coordination among the 38 universities and community colleges in the state. He came to Florida from the University of Maine system where he served for eight years as Dean of Information Technologies and Telecommunications for the Education Network of Maine. His academic degrees are in telecommunications, education, and public administration.

Marie L. Kotter (Chapter 7) is Vice President for Student Services at Weber State University (WSU), a position she has held for 12 years. Weber State has offered distance learning degrees for several years, and they have recently initiated WSU On Line, which offers Web-based courses. Marie holds B. S. and M. S. degrees in clinical laboratory science and a Ph. D. in educational psychology from the University of Utah. She has written three books and several articles, and she has given numerous workshops and presentations related to student services and medical technology issues.

Barbara Krauth (Chapter 1) is directing a project designed to improve student services for distance learners at the Western Cooperative for Educational Telecommunications, a program of the Western Interstate Commission for Higher Education (WICHE). Barbara leads a "double" professional life. In addition to her work in higher education, she is also a consultant and researcher in the field of criminal justice. Barbara has a B. A. in English from Indiana University, graduate hours in public administration at the University of Colorado, and an M. A. in English literature from the University of Kent, Canterbury, England.

John Witherspoon (Chapter 4) is Professor Emeritus and former Chair of Telecommunications and Film in the School of Communication, San Diego State University. A planner and consultant in telecommunication, he specializes in applications of communication technology for education and public service. John was founding Chairman of the Steering Committee of the Western Cooperative for Educational Telecommunications. He is the author of *Distance Education: A Planner's Casebook,* intended to assist higher education administrators as they look beyond the campus-bound university. Earlier, John was President of the Public Service Satellite Consortium, the first principal executive for television of the Corporation for Public Broadcasting, Vice President of KCET Los Angeles, and the first General Manager of KPBS-TV/FM, San Diego's public broadcasting stations. He was founding Chairman of the Board of Directors of National Public Radio.

of Maine system whom he served for eight years. Dean of the mudd... facilities and telecommunications in the Education Network of Maine. His academic degrees are in telecommunications and public administration.

Acknowledgments

This Guide was the brainchild of Sally Johnstone, Director of the Western Cooperative for Educational Telecommunications. It was she who initiated discussions with Prentice Hall that led to their enthusiastic support of this project, and it was Sally who chose the team of authors who wrote the book. She worked with us at every stage of the development of the manuscript and on each of the myriad production decisions that must be made when producing a book. Without Sally this book would not have been published.

A number of colleagues assisted us by reviewing the first draft of each chapter. Their perceptive comments about the content and suggestions for revision were instrumental in improving the final manuscript. Our sincere appreciation goes to the following reviewers:

Larry G. Benedict, Dean
Homewood Student Affairs
Johns Hopkins University

Anton Camarota
University of Denver

Steven D. Crow, Executive Director
Commission on Institutions of Higher
    Education North Central Association

Betty Elliott, Associate Dean of
    Instruction
Rio Salado College

Charlotte Farr, Director
Distance Education
University of Nevada

Debbie Flodin, Coordinator, Career
    Services
University of Alaska

Elaine Gray
Valencia Community College

Jean Hernandez, Director
Center for Career Services
University of Washington

Janet Ross Kendall, Director
External Degree Program
Washington State University

John E. Kobara, President
The Home Education Network (THEN)

David Lassner, Director
Information Technology Services
University of Hawaii

Christine L. Legore, Associate Director
Academic and Student Support Services
University of Maine System Network for
    Education and Technology Services

Mark Resmer, Associate Vice President
Sonoma State University

Richard O. Schafer, Director of Flexible
    Learning
University of Wisconsin

Maureen Schlenker
University of Colorado–Denver

Nancy Stegall
DeVry Institute of Technology–Phoenix

Terri Taylor Straut, Director
Customer and Provider Relations
Western Governors University

Danelle Thompson
Colorado School of Mines

Nancy Thompson
University of Georgia

Ellen Waterman
Regis University

Susan Barnes Whyte, Librarian
Northrup Library
Linfield College

Vicky York, Associate Professor
The Libraries
Montana State University

Four colleagues provided incalculable help by reviewing the entire draft manuscript:

H. Draper Hunt, Professor Emeritus
University of Southern Maine

Robert Threlkeld, Dean
Learning and Technology
California State University

Steve Tilson, Director, Distance Learning
Front Range Community College

Ellen Wagner, Vice President
Infomania

We also wish to thank the following current and former students who read parts or all of the manuscript and offered valuable suggestions for revising and strengthening various sections:

Marcie Bowden

Val Greene

Linda Kennedy

Kandis Novatny

Scott Olin, Dickinson

Christopher Padilla

Linda Silvia

Jan Todd

Jacqueline Hall

Ashley Ceisr

Todd Diehl

Jason Schierkolk

We owe a special debt to Paul Albright who did a masterful job editing the final draft of the manuscript. We appreciate his flexibility and his ability to pull together all of the parts of very complicated subject matter.

We are indebted to Daniel Cave and Jennifer Carbajal, staff at the Western Cooperative for Educational Telecommunications; both provided enormous assistance by coordinating deadlines and numerous mailings among authors and handling the multitude of details necessary to bring this book to completion.

A special thanks to the members of the Western Cooperative for Educational Telecommunications for their support of the collective efforts that are reflected in this book.

Finally, we would like to thank several people at Prentice Hall who helped to make this book happen. First and foremost, our sincere thanks to Carol Carter, our publisher, who has been enormously helpful at all stages of the development of the book. She has provided guidance and help when it was needed. Kevin Johnson's energy and ideas have inspired us from our first discussions with Prentice Hall, from book concept to design and layout. Pat Henry Leonard, President of Distance Learning, helped us to shape our vision for the book and the web site. Our production staff, Mary Carnis, Pat Walsh, Gay Pauley, and Marianne Frasco, worked under extremely tight deadlines and did a superb job.

Index